Žižek's 'The Sublime Object of Ideology'

BLOOMSBURY READER'S GUIDES

Titles available in this series

Aristotle's 'Politics': A Reader's Guide, Judith A. Swanson
Badiou's 'Being and Event': A Reader's Guide, Christopher Norris
Berkeley's 'Principles of Human Knowledge': A Reader's Guide, Alasdair Richmond
Deleuze's 'Difference and Repetition': A Reader's Guide, Joe Hughes
Deleuze and Guattari's 'A Thousand Plateaus': A Reader's Guide, Eugene W. Holland
Deleuze and Guattari's 'What is Philosophy': A Reader's Guide, Rex Butler
Descartes' 'Meditations': A Reader's Guide, Richard Francks
Hegel's 'Phenomenology of Spirit': A Reader's Guide, Stephen Houlgate
Heidegger's 'Being and Time': A Reader's Guide, William Blattner
Hobbes's 'Leviathan': A Reader's Guide, Laurie M. Johnson Bagby
Kant's 'Critique of Aesthetic Judgement': A Reader's Guide, Fiona Hughes
Kierkegaard's 'Fear and Trembling': A Reader's Guide, Clare Carlisle
Levinas' 'Totality and Infinity': A Reader's Guide, William Large
Locke's 'Second Treatise of Government': A Reader's Guide, Paul Kelly
Marx and Engels' 'Communist Manifesto': A Reader's Guide, Peter Lamb
Nietzsche's 'Beyond Good and Evil': A Reader's Guide, Christa Davis Acampora and Keith Ansell Pearson
Nietzsche's 'Thus Spoke Zarathustra': A Reader's Guide, Clancy Martin
Rousseau's 'The Social Contract': A Reader's Guide, Christopher Wraight
Spinoza's 'Ethics': A Reader's Guide, J. Thomas Cook
Wittgenstein's 'Philosophical Investigations': A Reader's Guide, Arif Ahmed
Wittgenstein's 'Tractatus Logico-Philosophicus': A Reader's Guide, Roger M. White
Heidegger's 'Being and Time': A Reader's Guide 2nd edition, William Blattner

Žižek's 'The Sublime Object of Ideology'

A Reader's Guide

Rafael Winkler

BLOOMSBURY ACADEMIC
LONDON • NEW YORK • OXFORD • NEW DELHI • SYDNEY

BLOOMSBURY ACADEMIC
Bloomsbury Publishing Plc
50 Bedford Square, London, WC1B 3DP, UK
1385 Broadway, New York, NY 10018, USA
29 Earlsfort Terrace, Dublin 2, Ireland

BLOOMSBURY, BLOOMSBURY ACADEMIC and the Diana logo are trademarks of Bloomsbury Publishing Plc

First published in Great Britain 2024

Series design by Catherine Wood
Cover image © VectorMine / Shutterstock

A catalogue record for this book is available from the British Library.

A catalog record for this book is available from the Library of Congress.

ISBN: HB: 978-1-3504-2564-4
PB: 978-1-3504-2565-1
ePDF: 978-1-3504-2566-8
eBook: 978-1-3504-2567-5

Series: Reader's Guides

Typeset by Deanta Global Publishing Services, Chennai, India
Printed and bound in Great Britain

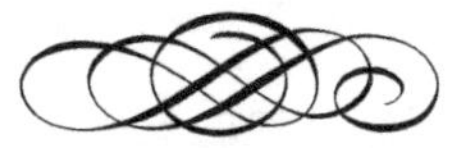

Contents

Acknowledgements vii
List of Abbreviations viii

1 Context 1
The Habermas-Foucault debate and Althusser 1
Laclau and Mouffe: Antagonism and the Real of the drive 7

2 Overview of themes 15
The critique of ideology 15
Subject-positions and antagonism 18
The reality and pleasure principles and the drive 20

3 Reading the text 25

Section 1 26
What is money? 26
Exchange: Alfred Sohn-Rethel 29
Cynical consciousness: Peter Sloterdijk 30
Belief and ideology 33
Althusser: Interpellation and misrecognition 36
Kant and the Law 42
Disidentification 45

Section 2 48
Retroactivity (*Nachträglichkeit*) 49
Error as the way to the truth 55
Desire and lack 59

Trauma redux 61
The form of ideology 62

Section 3 66
The constitution of sublime objects 66
The constitution of the subject and enjoyment (*jouissance*) 78

Section 4 92
Symbolic and physical existence: Symbolic and physical death 92
Benjamin's 'Theses on the Philosophy of History' 101
Power and its representation 108

Section 5 111
'There is no metalanguage': Derrida and dissemination 111
Lacan and 'Lenin in Warsaw' 116
The Real revisited 117
Freedom and the forced choice: the Real 120
Lack, the subject and the ontological inconsistency of the big Other 124
The ideological function of *objet a* 128
The subject presumed to . . . 130

Section 6 132
The indefinite judgement, lack and negation 132
Beauty and the sublime: The pleasure principle and its beyond 138
From Kant to Hegel: Lack and negativity 142
'Spirit is a bone' 144
Hegel's *Phenomenology of Spirit* and the heroism of flattery 146
The 'beautiful soul' and positing the presuppositions 149

4 Reception and influence 155

Notes 159
Select Bibliography 162
Index 164

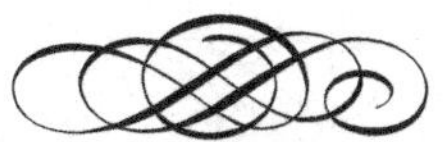

Acknowledgements

This project began as a reading group in early 2023. We'd meet for two hours every Friday at 11.00 AM at the IT Corner on the corner of 7th Street and 3rd Avenue in Melville, Johannesburg, for a period of three months. Our aim was to understand the intricacies and unravel the complexities of Žižek's Lacanian rehabilitation of the Marxist notion of ideology in *The Sublime Object of Ideology*. The notes I prepared and distributed weekly constituted the first draft of what eventually became this Reader's Guide to Žižek's text.

I want to take this opportunity to thank everyone who participated in the weekly reading group, including Chad Harris, Asheel Singh, Catherine Otto, Chantelle Gray, Aragorn Eloff, Yolanda and Yoliswa Mlungwana, Reneilwe Masuluke and Dominic Griffiths. The better parts of this work is due to our conversations.

I want to thank the Department of Philosophy at the University of Johannesburg for allowing me to complete this project in the tranquility of my home in the last two months of semester 1 of 2023.

Finally, to Salomé and Mira, all I can say is that the world would be a grim and sad place without the lightness and joy you bring to it.

Abbreviations

The following include Žižek's works cited below:

SOI *The Sublime Object of Ideology* (Verso: London, UK and New York, USA, 2008).

CHU *Contingency, Hegemony, University: Contemporary Dialogues on the Left* (Verso: London, UK, New York, US, 2000).

NEP *For They Know not What They Do: Enjoyment as a Political Factor* (Verso: London, UK, and New York, USA, 2008).

ES *Enjoy Your Symptom! Jacques Lacan in Hollywood and out* (Routledge: New York, London, 1992).

PV *The Parallax View* (The MIT Press: Cambridge, Massachusetts, London, England, 2006).

ZR *The Žižek Reader*, ed. E. Wright and E. Wright (Blackwell Publishing: MA, USA, Oxford, UK, Victoria, Australia, 2005).

SE *Surplus-Enjoyment: A Guide for the Non-Perplexed* (Bloomsbury Academic: London, New York, 2022)

PF *The Plague of Fantasies* (Verso: London and New York, 2008).

TN *Tarrying with the Negative: Kant, Hegel, and the Critique of Ideology* (Duke University Press: Durham, 1998)

1

Context

The Habermas-Foucault debate and Althusser

Slavoj Žižek's *The Sublime Object of Ideology* (his first book in English) appears in 1989. Four years earlier, Jürgen Habermas publishes *The Philosophical Discourse of Modernity* in which he defends a version of the Enlightenment project against such critics of modernity as Nietzsche, Bataille and Foucault (among others) who see in it moral nihilism, decadence and so on, instead of progress, the acquisition of rights and freedoms, the liberation of mankind from the oppressive forces of tradition and capitalism and so on. Habermas is out to defend the value of reason or of a communicative rationality that underpins modern participatory democratic institutions, against those whom he perceives to be a threat to the process of democratization on account of their skepticism of and mistrust in reason. Foucault dies in 1984, the year before Habermas' book comes out, and one of the debates raging in academia at the time – the time being the decade of the 1980s until, at the end of the 1980s and during the 1990s, deconstruction comes to dominate the academic scene in the English-speaking world – is whether Foucault's Nietzsche-inspired genealogical analysis of disciplinary practices or Habermas' Hegel-inspired communicative rationality offers a more incisive critique of the power relations permeating modern society. You'd hear at conferences or read in papers, edited volumes, journals or books that Foucault offers you insights on the constitution of the economically useful and politically obedient subject via the deployment of disciplines in institutions like the school, the hospital, the prison and so on, but that he robs you of the normative standpoint from which you can say whether such-or-such institutions, such-or-such actions are good or bad. As Foucault says somewhere, there is nothing in society that is good or bad, but everything is dangerous. In contrast, Habermas' approach provides you with just such an immanent normative-evaluative standpoint – immanent, that is, to the failing practice or institution in question – a standpoint that makes it possible to determine with others and by means of agreed upon rational principles the merit of the practice or institution in terms of its proposed goals. But the commentator or speaker would go on, his model of power is inadequate. Not only does it fail to capture its capillary structure in modern society. It also relies upon the timeworn top-down model: there are oppressors and there are the oppressed and the experience of power, of its force or violence, is like that of the boot of the SS officer squashing its victim's jowl. Habermas does not appear to have an inkling of the fact that power is productive, that it constitutes the subject by attaching bodies to an identity, type or clinically determined desire and so on (pathological/normal, perverse/neurotic/psychotic). Žižek opens the Introduction of his book with this very debate between Habermas and Foucault in order to show that it hides a neglected alternative: the Lacan-Althusser axis.

> There is something enigmatic in the sudden eclipse of the Althusserian school: it cannot be explained away in terms of a theoretical defeat. It is more as if there were, in Althusser's theory, a traumatic kernel which had to be quickly forgotten, 'repressed'; it is an effective case of theoretical amnesia. (SOI xxiii-xxiv)

Althusser's theory calls into question an assumption shared by both Foucault and Habermas. This is that there are strategies the subject can use to neutralize certain effects of power, that the subject can be rescued from the ideological grid, or, what amounts to the same thing, that an ideologically neutral subject is, politically speaking, not impossible. Of course, such a shared assumption should be infinitely qualified and refined. It goes without saying that the ideal subject for Habermas and Foucault isn't the same – though, and this is the point, they do have an ideal, one that has liberated itself from oppressive forms of power or from immobilized, fixed power relations. Habermas' ideal subject is the self-transparent intersubjective community that has achieved consensus on matters of justice, right and law, whereas according to Žižek, Foucault's is the subject that fashions herself in the way an author fashions her characters in a novel. She is someone who creates herself, her sexual or gender identity, who gives shape to her vices and virtues, who gives her character style and so on by using the resources and techniques available in the social field. Žižek detects in Foucault's ideal, beyond Nietzsche's 'sovereign individual', the humanist Renaissance agent who masters his passions and shapes his existence as if it were a work of art.[1] One way of putting this is to say that there is still hope in Habermas and Foucault (obviously more so in Habermas than in Foucault) and it is this hope tied to the belief in the ideologically emancipated subject that is belied by Althusser's theory of interpellation. For, according to the latter, there is no way out of ideology or, more precisely, ideology doesn't consist simply in the reification of the social relation (i.e. labour), it doesn't consist merely in making you see your labour power as just another commodity on the market to be sold for a price. Ideology for Althusser is a mechanism of subjectivation, it constitutes the subject. An 'ideologically-neutral subject' is on this view a contradiction in terms. Or better yet, if you were to shed your 'ideological glasses', you'd find yourself stripped of the big Other, that is, of the symbolic order that sustains your position as a subject for the world.

Ideology for Žižek is ubiquitous. It coincides with the symbolic order. It exists not simply out there in the world in structural inequalities whose injustice tends to be masked and rendered innocuous. It prevails as well in your deepest, most private thoughts and fantasies. I am reminded of an episode in Don DeLillo's *White Noise* where one of Jack Gladney's daughters says out loud in her sleep at night in bed, *Toyota Corolla*, *Toyota Celica*, *Toyota Cressida*, as if the market had colonized her unconscious. Nothing limits ideology-cum-the symbolic order save the Real of the drive. That is why the radical act for Žižek is the act of 'subjective destitution'. The critique of ideology demands nothing less than that I sacrifice my position as subject – that is, my attachment to the symbolic order. It demands an act of symbolic suicide, an ethical gesture. It is not simply a question of dis-identifying with the desire of the Other in order to forge my own desire (separation). It is a matter of suspending the belief that the big Other – society, the symbolic order – exists. The supposition that it exists makes my experiences consistent and meaningful. By neutralizing it, I embrace my experiences in their contingency and meaninglessness, and I am led to affirm the stupidity of the drive (the Real) that they ceaselessly border on, confront and occlude.

> [I]t is clear that the whole of [Althusser's] work embodies a certain radical ethical attitude which we might call the heroism of alienation or of subjective destitution. (SOI xxv; word added by me)

In Žižek's eyes, the end of the critique of ideology coincides with the end of the psychoanalytic cure and, thus, not with 'science' as traditionally conceived in classical Marxism and Althusser. We will see in Section 1 why Žižek thinks that one gets out of ideology not by means of the knowledge that exposes its illusions but thanks to an ethical gesture, or, indeed, therapeutically. This ethical dimension gives Žižek's critique of ideology an existential dimension. It is enough here to recall the fact that the locus of ideology, the site where it operates, is, according to Althusser, not so much the market as the subject. The principal effect of ideology is subjectivation, the transformation of what Althusser calls the 'individual', which is something indeterminate like Aristotle's *prima materia*, into a subject, that is, someone with a determinate social identity who thinks of herself as an agent.

The point I have been insisting on is that according to Žižek, the differences between Habermas and Foucault are secondary if we look at them from the point of view of Althusser's theory of interpellation. The latter questions their shared assumption. The 'real break is represented by Althusser, by his insistence on the fact that a certain cleft, a certain fissure, misrecognition, characterizes the human condition as such: by the thesis that the idea of the possible end of ideology is an ideological idea par excellence' (SOI xxiv). What is there a misrecognition of? It can be glossed, in the first instance, as the error of naturalizing a social relation. The State or one of its apparatuses, for example, the school I was sent to as a child, addresses me as male, white, Jewish and so on, and I take these inherently social mandates as natural, inborn, God-given and so on, as if I had always been that. The 'process of ideological interpellation through which the subject "recognizes" itself as the addressee in the calling up of the ideological cause implies necessarily a certain short circuit, an illusion of the type "I was already there'" (SOI xxv). Naturally I might question these qualities attributed to me. I might refuse to be labeled as such ('No, I don't consider myself Jewish anymore') or I might contest the current interpretation of these labels ('No, to be Jewish doesn't mean that you *de facto* support the actions of the Israeli government,' etc.). Still, it is insofar as this misrecognition has taken place that I can take a reflexive attitude towards the signifiers with which I identify: misrecognition is unavoidable.

At a formal level, there is a misrecognition of what I take myself to be when I identify as subject: I take myself to be an *agent* – the agent of my thoughts and actions, of history or of destiny and so on. The truth is that the subject is an effect of interpellation, and it is as unavoidable that I misrecognize myself as an agent as that I misrecognize myself in terms of such concrete social roles. As we will see, this is the central aspect of imaginary identification. To be an agent, an autonomous, autarchic being, is my Ideal Ego. It is what, in the final analysis, I want to be for the big Other, that is, in order to be likeable to it.

> The point is not just that we must unmask the structural mechanism which is producing the effect of subject as ideological misrecognition, but that we must at the same time fully acknowledge this misrecognition as unavoidable – that is, we must accept a certain delusion as a condition of our historical activity, of assuming the role as agent of the historical process. (SOI xxv)

Misrecognition is unavoidable. It is where the human being begins. It begins alienated in the symbolic order. Alienated? Yes, but not in the classical Marxist sense according to which I am alienated from my essence on entering a commodity-producing society, that is, capitalism, or in the sense that the market suppresses and hides my freedom or species-being. Alienation in Lacan's sense has nothing to do with the notion that my essence is occluded by the established order. It is similar to the concept of thrownness in Heidegger's *Being and Time*. Before I can even say 'I am so-and-so' to the person hailing me in the street, I find myself in a world – a language, culture, tradition, political regime and so on – I have not created and that is not mine and that is accordingly other and alien. I am hailed by all of these things – language, culture, tradition and so on – through the other person that embodies for me the big Other. The big Other for Lacan is the symbolic order. It is not identical to 'the world' in the phenomenological sense: the horizon of meaning and focal point for the projection of my existence. It is a system of signifiers lacking substantiality and life. It is a 'dead letter', a machine that generates sense, a formal, timeless structure that renders transparent the contingent and imaginary contents of culture, language and so on. More on this later. For now, let me just say that in talking about 'where the human being begins', I do not mean its natural beginning at birth or during conception. The subject's symbolic identity is determined *prior* to birth or conception. It is *determined by the name* (the signifier) *that anticipates its physical existence*, the name the infant will inherit and bear, the father's name and, thus, the Name-of-the-Father in societies where patrilineal descent is the norm. This is just another way of saying that ideology – the symbolic order – is almost all-enveloping. I say 'almost' because, as I have begun to suggest and will explain at greater length later on, its limit is the Real of the drive, not some fact in the empirical world but, instead, the unsymbolized and unsymbolizable, the trauma that recurs precisely to the extent that it refuses to be symbolically digested and integrated.

One more word on interpellation. How does it work? Althusser's model is the following. A person in authority says 'Hey you!' Is he calling someone in particular? It doesn't matter. The point is that the person who turns round identifies with the call and is interpellated under that name. The signifier sticks to him because he accepts it. He identifies with it. What needs to be noted is that the signifier wouldn't stick unless the caller were someone who embodies the authority of the symbolic order. Anyone can tell me who I am, those I consider my equals and those whom I see as authority figures. The signifier that determines my being issues from an authority figure, my parents or caregivers, as well as my teachers, state functionaries or representatives of an institution, a club, race, ethnicity, religion and so on. The power he has over me is unique: he tells me (of course, obliquely, indirectly!) who I need to be in order to belong and be worthy of his love or respect. (We will see later on that this is the central feature of symbolic identification: I want to be worthy of his love and to that end, I become the representative of this order, cast, ethnicity, club, etc.)

Laclau and Mouffe: Antagonism and the Real of the drive

In the next two pages of the Introduction (SOI xxvi-xxvii), Žižek begins to introduce one of the core arguments of *The Sublime Object of Ideology*. He positions himself against the foundationalism of classical Marxism and the post-structuralism of Ernesto Laclau and Chantal Mouffe's *Hegemony and Socialist Strategy: Towards a Radical Democratic Politics* by arguing that the traumatic Real is what all antagonisms in society are of. Žižek spells out his argument in 'Beyond Discourse-Analysis'.

Let me clarify the sense in which Marxism is a foundationalist doctrine. Let's start with the uncontroversial observation that we find in society a multiplicity of conflicts. The feminist fights for the rights of women, the ecologist fights against the exploitation of nature, the worker's party fights for the rights of workers, 'democrats for political and social freedoms' and so on. The classical Marxist insists that there is one conflict that is fundamental and the basis of all the others. This is the class conflict, that between labour and capital, the proletarians and the owners of the means of production. The claim is that by resolving the class conflict, all the others will also be resolved. There will be equal pay in the workplace, the exploitation of nature will be over and so on, once the class conflict is resolved. The latter is the ground of the others. As long as it persists, they too persist. This is why Marx takes the class conflict to be the basis of history. What causes history to move is the contradiction between social classes. By the same token, history comes to an end with the resolution of the class conflict. That is in fact the goal of history. History aims at the institution of a rationally governed society, a society that is at one with itself, notably, communism.

Laclau and Mouffe break with this view of history as well as with the idea that the economy is the explanatory basis of surface phenomena like politics, religion, literature and the like. In their eyes, politics is war by other means. Conflict is irreducible and the idea of a closed, harmonious society that is transparent to itself is the very substance of ideology.

For Laclau and Mouffe, it's a question of politicizing one's struggle. As Žižek puts it, 'almost any of the antagonisms which, in light of Marxism, appear to be secondary can take over this essential role of mediator for all the others'. (SOI xxvii) You have to stake your particular struggle – whether for workers' rights, women's equal pay, the environment and so on – as one that is of universal interest. You make a part stand for the whole, that is, you 'hegemonize' your struggle. Politics involves putting forth your struggle as one whose resolution will bring about the public good, that is, a harmonious society, against other agents who see the resolution of *their* struggle as the way to bring about the public good. This contestation between social agents is what radical democracy looks like. Doing anything else, like lobbying the State for advancing the private interests of groups and corporations as in the United States and countries where the liberal tradition is strong, is inherently depoliticizing. In a situation where politics is alive in the sense described, we have a democratic contestation between a plurality of social actors whose view of society – of the common good, the *res publica* – is incommensurable. There is no common ground between the views of society on the Left and Right. The position of each excludes the position of the others. This is one reason why society as a perfectly harmonious, all-inclusive totality is impossible. It remains a representation – a chain of signifiers – rather than something realized in fact (or outside of language).

In Žižek's eyes, Laclau and Mouffe fall short in their leaning toward 'post-structuralism'.

> Lacanian psychoanalysis goes a decisive step further than the usual 'post-Marxist' anti-essentialism affirming the irreducible plurality of particular struggles – in other words, demonstrating how their articulation into a series of equivalences depends always on the radical contingency of the social-historical process: it enables us to grasp this plurality as a multitude of responses to the same impossible-real kernel. (SOI xxvii)

What Žižek objects to is best explained in reference to Laclau's short 1983 essay 'The Impossibility of Society' which contains the principal argument of *Hegemony and Socialist Strategy: Towards a Radical Democratic Politics*. It will assist us in understanding the alternative Žižek proposes, notably, that social conflicts do in fact have a quasi-foundation. It is not, to be sure, the economy, but the limit of the symbolic order, the Real of the drive.

Laclau begins his essay by reporting two claims from orthodox Marxism. The first is that ideology exists at a certain (superstructural) level of society, the second is that ideology signifies false consciousness. The first notion was undermined when the assumption on which it was based was called into question by structuralism and, to a greater extent, by Derrida: that society is an intelligible totality whose parts and relations, whose levels, can be identified; the second was likewise undermined when the idea of human agency was called into question, that is, that freedom is the essence of the human being. Laclau writes that 'the two approaches were grounded in an *essentialist* conception of both society and social agency'.[2]

As concerns the first, the conception of society as a totality operates in science 'as an underlying principle of intelligibility of the social order'. The totality is the essence of society that has to be recognized behind the empirical variation at the surface of social life. As opposed to this notion, Laclau follows the Derridean view in affirming '*the infinitude of the social*'. Society is equated with discourse and discourse, in turn, cannot be limited by something non-discursive, yet if not by something non-discursive then it cannot be limited at all. It is always bleeding meaning. It is impossible to contain or limit the movement of signification. A signifier signifies other signifiers. Any 'structural system' is 'always surrounded by an "excess of meaning" which it is unable to master' and, consequently, '"society" as a unitary and intelligible object which grounds its own partial processes is an impossibility'. For structuralism, social identity is relational. It has no positive content of its own. It is determined by neighboring identities. This is the great step taken by structuralism. The second step is taken by deconstruction. If identity has a relational character and it cannot be fixed once and for all, 'then the social must be identified with the infinite play of differences, that is, with what in the strictest sense of the term we can call discourse – on the condition, of course, that we liberate the concept of discourse from its restrictive meaning as speech and writing'. Laclau reinvests the meaning of society beyond its classical conception in Marxism. Society = Discourse = Open-Ended Chain of Differential Elements (signifiers).

Of course, a discourse where meaning cannot be fixed is psychotic and unintelligible. That is why Laclau continues by insisting that politics (or the 'social', as he calls it in the essay) is the attempt to arrest the movement of signification, to fix a meaning by means of 'nodal points'. In *Hegemony and Socialist Strategy: Towards a Radical Democratic Politics*, these 'nodal points' become Lacan's 'quilting points', as we will see when we approach Chapter 2 of *The Sublime Object of Ideology*. The fundamental political operation is to temporarily limit the infinite play of differences (discourse) by endowing a particular signifier with an exorbitant value in such a way that neighboring signifiers cluster around it, as if it enveloped their meaning. It is a matter of '*hegemonizing*' discourse. It goes without saying that such attempts are precarious. For Laclau, politics is a pragmatism of discourse. There are no eternal laws, there is nothing *a priori*. It is a question of identifying, in the here and now, the relevant signifiers that can be made to work and evoke the universal interest.

Laclau further insists that the framework in which the notion of false consciousness made sense has, for various reasons, been undermined. It is not the case that the subject misrecognizes its true identity (for it has no true identity). The social identity of agents is as differentially determined as the elements of discourse. We must start from the position that the subject is decentered,

> that his/her identity is nothing but the unstable articulation of constantly changing positionalities. The same excess of meaning, the same precarious character of any structuration that we find in the domain of the social order, is also to be found in the domain of subjectivity. But if any social agent is a decentered subject, if when attempting to determine his/her identity we find nothing else but kaleidoscopic movement of differences, in what sense can we say that subjects misrecognize themselves? The point is that we cannot. They do not misrecognize their identity because they do not have an immutable, natural or metaphysical one to begin with.

Instead of getting rid of the notion of ideology as false consciousness, however, Laclau proposes that we think differently about it. Ideology doesn't mean falsifying the consciousness of my self. It means falsifying the consciousness of society. To see society as a positivity, as a set of empirical facts existing out there that can be combined in various ways; to see it as a totality, whether given or completed, or to misrecognize the precarious and temporary character of the nodal points that suture the infinite play of differences in a finite whole – all this is ideology.

> The ideological would consist of those discursive forms through which a society tries to institute itself as such on the basis of closure, of the fixation of meaning, of the non-recognition of the infinite play of differences. The ideological would be the will to 'totality' of any totalizing discourse. And insofar as the social is impossible without some fixation of meaning, without the discourse of closure, the ideological must be seen as constitutive of the social. The social only exists as the vain attempt to institute that impossible object: society.[3]

There is no 'society' – a common public space, objectivity, the big Other and so on – without the use of nodal points that temporarily arrest the sliding of the signified under the signifier. There has to be a signifier that *refers to itself as the signifier of the whole*. There has to be a master or phallic signifier, be it 'communism', 'democracy' or something else that stitches up the field of discourse in a closed whole. That is to say that society exists to the extent that its temporary suture is misrecognized and the whole is taken for a closed totality or essence that manifests itself variously at the empirical level. In one word, ideology is unavoidable.

Žižek accepts most of the results of Laclau's analysis. What he objects to is the Derridean view according to which the play of differences is unlimited. Yes, particular social conflicts are linked to one another – they are articulated into a 'series of equivalences' – by reference to a nodal point that has the character of a foundation for them. Yes, they are grounded by a political agent in a particular conflict that she takes to be the fundamental one, the key to resolving the others. But the fundamental antagonism is for Žižek *not another social conflict*, it is the deadlock of the Real, of, precisely, what escapes discourse and the play of the signifier. At bottom, discourse breaks down where it encounters trauma. It is not a bad metaphor to say that the symbolic order 'turns round' the Real, bodily *jouissance*, the Freudian drive and so on. The truth is that the Real disturbs the movement of signification by compulsively returning, and it returns precisely because it remains unsymbolized. You repeat what you cannot remember (Freud), what, in other words, you cannot represent, signify, symbolically institute or integrate in the infinite movement of referral and difference. We should recall here the central insight of *The Sublime Object of Ideology*. This deadlock of the drive that prevents the subject from coinciding with itself, from being at one with itself and whole, is projected outwards in the other, for example, in the foreigner or Jew, in such a way that he is made responsible for the fact that the subject – or, in effect, society – is not at one with itself, harmonious and whole. More on this later.

Žižek makes it clear that by the 'Freudian drive' or 'death drive' he doesn't mean some biological instinct or compulsion to see all things ruined. The death drive isn't after death, destruction or mayhem. It is a 'blind automatism of repetition' (SOI xxvii) that upends the homeostatic balance of the living being and that violates the pleasure principle. On the one hand, the pleasure and reality principles are, on this Lacanian picture, taken to be in the service of the imperative of life: adaptation, survival, conformity and so on. They are there to ensure stability which, for Freud, always means the same thing: whatever tensions may have built up in the organism over time, they have to be discharged as quickly and as efficiently as possible; the quantity of excitations, that is, the tension in the living being, has to be lessened or kept to a minimum and constant level. On the other hand, the drive demands satisfaction and because this demand is, like Kant's categorical imperative, unconditional (in Žižek's terms, 'blind' or 'stupid'), satisfying it can go the length of endangering the living being. It can bring the subject to abandon its attachment to life, as happens, for instance, when it values something above (its) life. I don't mean freedom only, as in the common revolutionary cry *Liberty or Death!* but also love, the Lady in the medieval rituals of courtly love for whose sake the prince-and-lover is ready to sacrifice his wealth and life. I am also thinking of one of Žižek's heroines in *The Sublime Object of Ideology*, Antigone who, unconsciously identifying with the death drive, willingly and knowingly goes to her death to bury her brother Polynices and perform the customary mourning rites. In each of these cases – freedom, love, subjective destitution through identification with the death drive – we witness something sublime, something that at the same time fascinates and disgusts us, in other words, something whose value transcends life and the subject's wellbeing.

In Freudian terms, the ego – that is, the agency in control of bodily motility – aims for adaptation, whereas the id causes it trouble. It wreaks havoc on account of its unconditional insistence on satisfaction. It leads to a kind of pleasure in displeasure. It leads to a heightening of tension, to an increase of excitations in the organism. The drive makes impossible whatever hoped-for harmony one has in view with regards to the relation between the human being and nature, society, others and so on. It is a source of ongoing instability. This is '*la condition humaine* as such: there is no solution, no escape from it; the thing to do is not to "overcome", to "abolish" it, but to come to terms with it, to learn to recognize it in its terrifying dimension and then, on the basis of this fundamental recognition, to try to articulate a *modus vivendi* with it' (SOI xxvii-xxviii). Žižek suggests that the totalitarian temptation is to abolish this source of tension: 'the greatest mass murders and holocausts have always been perpetrated in the name of man as harmonious being, of a New Man without antagonistic tension' (SOI xxviii).

* * *

Žižek concludes his Introduction by highlighting the three aims of *The Sublime Object of Ideology*.

(a) The aim is to show, against the usual post-structuralist picture of Lacanian psychoanalysis, that it is best understood 'in the lineage of rationalism'.

(b) The aim is also to provide an alternative to the common picture of Hegel as an idealist and monist where reason, as it were, swallows whole its other by infusing it with its rationality and transparency. On Žižek's reading of Hegel, '"absolute knowledge" itself is nothing but a name for the acknowledgment of a certain radical loss' (SOI xxx).

(c) Lastly, the book serves as an introduction to the theory of ideology.

In the following sections and chapters, I focus chiefly on Žižek's last aim.

2

Overview of themes

By way of situating some of the themes of *The Sublime Object of Ideology*, I want to provide a reading of Žižek's 'Beyond Discourse-Analysis'. It is a short essay written on the occasion of a conference organized by the Institute for Marxist Studies of the Slovenian Academy of Arts and Sciences in October 1987, two years before the publication of *The Sublime Object of Ideology*. The conference coincided with the publication of the Slovenian edition of Laclau and Mouffe's *Hegemony and Socialist Strategy: Towards a Radical Democratic Politics*. The presentations were mostly devoted to it. So was Žižek's essay. It contains the main insights of *The Sublime Object of Ideology*. I read it in conjunction with some of Žižek's remarks on the pleasure and reality principles and the drive in Freud in *Enjoy Your Symptom! Jacques Lacan in Hollywood and Out!* (1992).

The critique of ideology

Žižek prefaces 'Beyond Discourse-Analysis' by emphasizing what is novel in Laclau and Mouffe's *Hegemony and Socialist Strategy: Towards a Radical Democratic Politics*. This is that the symbolic order ineluctably gravitates around what it forecloses, that is, the Real of the drive. Far

> from reducing all reality to a kind of language-game, the socio-symbolic field is conceived as structured around a certain traumatic impossibility, around a certain fissure which *cannot* be symbolized. In short, Laclau and Mouffe have, so to speak, reinvented the Lacanian notion of the Real as

impossible, they have made it useful as a tool for social and ideological analysis.[1]

Žižek's principal claim is that there is a structural homology between social antagonism in Laclau and Mouffe and the Real in Lacan. To understand the position Žižek forges for himself, I situate it in the context of the debate between the followers of the 'unfinished project' of modernity (Habermasians) and the post-modern suspicion and distrust in reason. At stake is whether it is possible to delimit an extra-ideological space against ideologically constituted reality in order to legitimize the *critique* of ideology. It is the only place to my knowledge where Žižek tackles this issue head-on.

Let me begin with the general and well-founded claim that the Enlightenment is the promise of the liberation of mankind from the oppressive and arbitrary rule of scepter and censor, Church and King, through a critique of reason: what can reason rightly claim to know and do? The Enlightenment coincides with the consciousness that a rationally governed society is a liberated society, one unencumbered by superstitions and illusions in its pursuit of truth and right action. Human reason determines for itself the norms under which it knows and acts. Its limits are authored by it alone and to that extent, they are self-justifying, free and unconditional (not limited by anything external to it). A body of beliefs whose authority transcends reason and its ways of knowing is by that fact unlawful, arbitrary and violent. At any rate, that is how the adherent to the Enlightenment tradition sees matters. Any kind of interest – institutional, technical, moral or political – that distorts reason's emancipatory pursuits counts as ideological. For Habermas, for example, ideology is a systematically distorted communicative rationality. It is denounced in the name of a non-coercive transparent communication.

The post-modern critic, by contrast, by whom we mean, first of all, Nietzsche, Freud and (to a lesser extent) Marx, mistrusts reason, not only instrumental rationality and its inherent tendency to dominate nature and human beings but also purposive rationality, the rationality that sets forth a substantive notion of the good or of happiness. Foucault, for instance, insists on the fact that reason is plural – there are multiple rationalities and their function as disciplinary mechanisms is to form subjects who desire their own subjection. Reason does not liberate the subject. It forms the subject by subjecting the body to disciplinary mechanisms. For the post-modern critic, there is no ideologically neutral territory. Ideology is ubiquitous. But from what position of enunciation is it possible to utter such a claim? Isn't it possible to denounce discourse as ideological only from an ideologically *un*contaminated standpoint and discourse? But then the claim must be false that ideology is ubiquitous.

To summarize what I have said so far: for the Enlightenment thinker, ideology is the falsification of reality by various interests and prejudices, political, social, patriarchal and so on. For the post-modern critic, the idea that you have access to a reality unmediated by language or reason *qua* the symbolic order-cum-ideology is ideological. From the point of view of the post-modern critic, the Enlightenment thinker is naïve. He doesn't recognize the fact that the very attempt to distinguish between a falsified and non-falsified reality (or more generally, between appearance and truth) is *itself* ideological. The only non-ideological claim it seems possible to make, from the point of view of the post-modern critic, is that 'all is ideology'. But such a claim is false because it is not possible to denounce something as ideological except from a non-ideological standpoint. That is why Žižek contends that ideology is not all and that it is possible to take a distance from it. He is aware that the way to keep alive the *critique* of ideology is to maintain the tension between ideology and reality – that is, between ideologically constituted reality (the symbolic order) and the extra-ideological reality of the Real, of the thing foreclosed by the symbolic order that plagues the subject in the form of symptoms.

Because the traumatism of the drive (the Real) escapes the symbolic order (ideology), it is the standpoint from which it is possible to denounce as ideological the symbolic universes inhabited by subjects. A symptom is the site of the drive's enjoyment (*jouissance*). It is where it obtains satisfaction for the infantile-unconscious wishes outlawed by the social order. We can say that thought at bottom aims at the unthinkable or that language turns on the unsayable. The unsayable-unthinkable is the trauma the subject gravitates around. It is what ultimately *unmasks* the *inconsistency* and *lack* in the big Other, for it testifies to the fact that the symbolic order cannot integrate and signify it. The *critical* significance of the Real is that it exposes the inherent limit of the symbolic order as well as its non-natural, performative institution and origin.

Žižek defines the Real in 'Beyond Discourse-Analysis' as a deadlock in the structure of the drive, the very deadlock that makes it impossible, as a matter of principle, for the subject to coincide with itself. Now 'social antagonism' denotes the deadlock of the social in Laclau and Mouffe, the impossibility, as a matter of principle, for society to coincide with itself. Žižek's claim is thus that what Laclau and Mouffe call 'social antagonism' is structurally similar to Lacan's Real. Let me explain how the argument works.

Subject-positions and antagonism

Let me start with the theory of the subject in *Hegemony and Socialist Strategy*. We begin the analysis of a discursive formation with the subject-positions that it makes available. A subject-position – being a mother, daughter, banker and so on – is what a subject recognizes as part of her identity. It is defined by a mandate. Subject-positions behave like signifiers. They are determined, in their identity or meaning, negatively, that is, in their relations with one another. Consider in this context political subject-positions like that of the feminist, the democrat, the ecologist and so on. Laclau and Mouffe's claim is that their sense is determined by the way they are articulated with one another and form a united series. For example, the democrat finds that there is no democracy without the emancipation of women, that there is no reconciliation with nature without abandoning the aggressive-masculine attitude to nature and so on. Each position is determined in its content by all the others. Yet though together they make up a whole, it is a contingent one because each of these positions can be articulated differently with a variety of other subject-positions. Nothing rules out the possibility of combining the environmentalist position with an anti-democratic, authoritarian rule on the ground that the latter will get the job done and save humanity from environmental disaster. The series of equivalences are not an 'expression of some kind of internal necessity according to which all of the above-mentioned positions would in the long run "objectively convene." It is quite possible, for example, to imagine an ecological position which sees the only solution in a strong anti-democratic, authoritarian state resuming control over the exploitation of natural resources, etc.'[2]

Once we are constituted as ideological subjects, we are *a priori* deluded. We overlook social antagonism, that is, the trauma whose symbolization invariably fails. Each term in the antagonistic relation precludes the other from achieving its self-identity. The proletarian, for instance, struggles against the capitalist. In his eyes, the capitalist makes it impossible for him to realize his human potential. He blocks the proletarian's development as a human being. Where are we to situate the ideological illusion in this scene? The illusion is the proletarian's belief that by annihilating his enemy, he will abolish the antagonism and be free. He will coincide with himself and be happy. The same must be said of sexual antagonism. The feminist thinks that by dissolving patriarchy, women will finally realize their full identity as women. The truth is that it is not the enemy that blocks the subject from being himself; it is that self-identity is impossible, its realization is inwardly blocked. The external enemy is something upon which the subject projects this intrinsic limit. The enemy is for the subject an alibi. It is his way of evading the blockage of the drive. Put differently, repression in psychoanalysis (the formation of a symptom) *doesn't* coincide with the internalization of external-social oppression. The drive is hindered at the root. It is prevented from achieving satisfaction as a result of the fact that its object – the *objet a* – is lacking. Or rather, the drive *obtains* satisfaction precisely by circling around the forever-missing *objet a*, and the failure to possess it is projected on the external enemy. '*He* has it! *He* has stolen it from us.' The 'role of the fascinating figure of external Authority' is to make us blind to the self-impediment of the drive.

Žižek says in connection with the slave-master dialectic in Hegel's *Phenomenology of Spirit* that the slave liberates himself from the lord when he experiences how the lord was embodying the auto-blockage of his own desire: 'what the Lord through his external repression was supposed to deprive him of, to prevent him from realizing, he – the Bondsman – never possessed'.[3] The other embodies the subject's negative relation of the drive to itself. We can understand this in relation to the way Žižek takes Lacan's infamous 'woman is a symptom of man'. Why is she man's symptom? His identity depends on hers, it is defined by relation to hers, by her position in the social order. But she is unable to achieve self-identity (owing to the drive's deadlock). Hence, it is by foreclosing – or primordially repressing – her decentering/decentered position that he realizes his identity. You repress and compulsively repeat what you cannot signify. In that sense, '*woman' is the limit of the social order*. This is where Žižek's critical claim lies.

> We must then distinguish the experience of antagonism in its radical form, as a limit of the social, as the impossibility around which the social field is structured, from antagonism as the relation between antagonistic subject-positions: in Lacanian terms, we must distinguish antagonism as *real* from the social *reality* of the antagonistic fight.[4]

The difference is between the subject's encounter with the Real and the enemy. For Laclau and Mouffe, following Carl Schmidt, the political is where the difference is drawn between friend and enemy. It is the field of Laclau and Mouffe's radical democracy, the open-ended contestation between political agents who stake out different visions of the social order.

The encounter with the Real involves the subject losing his tie to the symbolic order: the whole of the social field strikes him as unbearable in its senseless and insistent presence. All that remains is the subject as 'empty place of the structure,'[5] that is, as the site of the missing Thing. This 'subject' – that is, the subject that identifies as *objet a* – is the inner limit of the big Other as well (and not only of the subject). It makes conspicuous its lack and inconsistency. If subjectivation has a *telos*, it is to obfuscate and make bearable the 'originary' trauma of the subject's submission to the signifier. The aim is to mask the drive's deadlock.

The reality and pleasure principles and the drive

Žižek's key idea is the drive's inner blockage. *Enjoy your Symptom! Jacques Lacan in Hollywood and Out!* contains a lucid description of the drive in its relation to the pleasure and reality principles. It moreover clarifies one of the central philosophical anthropological claims of *The Sublime Object of Ideology*.

Žižek writes at the end of the Introduction that the death drive 'defines *la condition humaine* as such: there is no solution, no escape from it; the thing to do is not to "overcome," to "abolish" it, but to come to terms with it, to learn to recognize it in its terrifying dimension and then, on the basis of this fundamental recognition, to try to articulate a *modus vivendi* with it'.

> All 'culture' is in a way a reaction-formation, an attempt to limit, canalize – to *cultivate* this imbalance, this traumatic kernel, this radical antagonism through which man cuts his umbilical cord with nature, with animal homeostasis. It is not only that the aim is no longer to abolish this drive antagonism, but the aspiration to abolish it is precisely the source of totalitarian temptation: the greatest mass murders and holocausts have always been perpetrated in the name of man as a harmonious being, of a New Man without antagonistic tension. (SOI xxviii)

Note the two important claims he makes. The drive is ineluctable; or, more precisely, because the drive is present in symptoms, at bottom Žižek is saying that you cannot liberate yourself from your symptoms. However, you can learn to live with them in such a way that they cease to oppress you. Second, the id is the agency through which 'man cuts his umbilical cord with nature'. Žižek posits the drive as the cause or principle of humanity's emergence from the state of nature. It is the non-natural, traumatic birth of culture and language, the symbolic order. Indeed, the symbolic order can be seen as attempting to make up for this traumatic breach and eternal separation from nature.

Pleasure too – and not only the id – sets the living being out of whack with nature. Freud posits a psychic apparatus whose chief principle puts it at odds with its natural environment. It runs after pleasure caring nothing for its consequences and for the limitations of reality. If it were to follow the immanent logic of the pleasure principle, the psychic apparatus would go to its ruin. The pursuit of pleasure unhindered by social taboos and the physical limitations of the human body would result in its destruction. The reality principle is installed in the psychic apparatus from without, that is, through the pressure of social taboos. Its function is to assure homeostatic balance. It is, further, the correlate of the ego, of the agency in control of bodily motility, which acts in the name of the living being's welfare. The demands of reality impose on it the renunciation of the absolute predominance of the pleasure principle and its transformation into the reality principle.

Freud introduces the concept of the drive in *Beyond the Pleasure Principle* to account for a variety of phenomena, including the patient's tendency to relive painful, traumatic experiences. This compulsive behavior conflicts with the pleasure principle and Freud claims that it is older than it. Consider dreams. A dream that fulfils a wish is under the governance of the pleasure principle. This is not the case of the dream of a patient who suffers a trauma. His dream does not fulfil a wish. It brings him back to the situation of his accident in order to master the surprise and shock that eluded him and that resulted in his trauma. The dream's aim is to master the excess after the fact and to develop the anxiety, that is, the defensive mechanism that would have prepared the patient and made it possible for him to withstand the shock. This entire operation 'must be accomplished before the dominance of the pleasure principle can even begin. [Such dreams] afford us a view of a function of the mental apparatus which, though it does not contradict the pleasure principle, is nevertheless independent of it and seems to be more primitive than the purpose of gaining pleasure and avoiding unpleasure'.[6] There is a horror and trauma older than the pleasure and reality principles. There is an incomprehensibility-enjoyment (*jouissance*) at the heart of life that life perpetually seeks to master but to no avail. The drive entails that satisfaction is impossible as a matter of principle. It is impossible not in the sense of being inconceivable or absurd. The thing that would fill the drive – the Thing or *objet a* – is missing.

> there is something in the very immanent functioning of the psyche, notwithstanding the pressure of 'external reality,' which resists full satisfaction. In other words, even if the psychic apparatus is entirely left to itself, it will not attain the balance for which the 'pleasure principle' strives, but it will continue to circulate around a traumatic intruder in its interior – the limit upon which the 'pleasure principle' stumbles is internal to it. (NEP 49)

The drive is a relentless and unconditional demand for satisfaction. It obtains satisfaction (*jouissance*) not by possessing the missing Thing but, instead, by constantly failing to attain it. There is pleasure in this displeasure. Enjoyment is always at the expense of the ego and its welfare (the reality principle). *It* enjoys when the subject fails to re-find the lost *a*.

Enjoyment (*jouissance*) can also be considered as a bodily intensity. As opposed to the pleasure principle, whose aim is to reduce to nil or keep constant the quantity of excitations in the mental apparatus, the drive's enjoyment (*jouissance*) adds to it fresh excitations, causing it displeasure. It is almost as if the goal were the continued intensification of the drive beyond what it is possible for the psychic apparatus to tolerate.

> the *objet a* prevents the circle of pleasure from closing, it introduces an irreducible displeasure, but the psychic apparatus finds a sort of perverse pleasure in *this displeasure itself*, in the never-ending repeated circulation around the unattainable, always missed object. (NEP 48)

The drive awakens the psychic apparatus – as Freud puts it in the *Interpretation of Dreams*, 'pain sets the apparatus in motion'[7] – and keeps the subject at a distance from itself or the symbolic order. This is why *dis*identification – the hysterical question 'Why am I what you say I am?' – is the subject's default position. The reverse side of the drive is the *lack* in the big Other. The Other lacks the *objet a*; and this lack, as noted before, is nothing but the empty place of the subject in the structure.

* * *

The Real, fantasy, the *objet a*, castration, the symbolic order – these are some of the themes that Žižek draws from Lacan in order to construct his Lacanian theory of ideology, along with a critical reading of Althusser on misrecognition and interpellation – themes that I propose to explore in the following Sections.

3

Reading the text

Section 1

In this section, my aim is to outline Žižek's argument in the first chapter of *The Sublime Object of Ideology*. It is not possible to address each one of his remarks. Instead, I show what he does with the concept of ideology and explain in what sense capitalism bears on money as a sublime object. A close treatment of the constitution of sublime objects is reserved for Section 3. In this section, I try to do justice to the way he mobilizes certain authors to advance his argument, and, at the end, I raise a few questions the student first approaching the text might want to keep in mind.

So, to begin with, what is ideology? What is it for Žižek? And in what sense are its objects sublime?

What is money?

Consider Žižek's discussion of money in the section titled 'The unconscious of the commodity-form'. Perhaps the first thing to note about money is that it is a peculiar kind of commodity. On the one hand, it is like any commodity something that is exchanged for goods. On the other hand, and at the same time, it embodies what Marx calls in Volume I of *Capital* the *general equivalent*. Money makes it possible to represent things in general as a value. Anything can be represented as a value, from milk to meat to nails to hair to body parts, you name it. We can go so far as to say that money alters the nature of what there is. What there is for the materialist are physical things. In relation to money, however, they become values, that is, commodities, that is, quantities of money, that is, nonsensuous abstract things.

Money is used to buy goods with. That is true. But money is not a use value in the strict sense Marx uses the expression. A use value is a good some of whose material properties are designed to satisfy a human need. It is a means to some end. A chair, a table, a spoon and so on, are use values. The material properties of money, the metal and paper from which coins and bills are made, are of no consequence. What matters is the *social function* it performs. Money is from the start something virtual or ideal; it is something purely symbolic. It is a State-produced and State-sanctioned medium of exchange. In this connection, any material would do. The existence of digital money today is the belated recognition of this fact – of the fact, namely, that money is at bottom something *immaterial*.

Everyone knows that the material used to make money (paper, metal, ink, etc.) is subject to wear and tear and that it is destined to be eventually destroyed. Yet we treat money as if its materiality were incorruptible, as if, instead of being subject to time, it were imperishable like the immaterial Forms of Plato's philosophy. The fetishistic tendency consists in hypostatizing its immaterial-social function.

> we know very well that money, like all other material objects, suffers the effects of use, that its material body changes through time, but in the social *effectivity* of the market we none the less *treat* coins as if they consist 'of an immutable substance, a substance over which time has no power, and which stands in antithetic contrast to any matter found in nature'.

It's as if money were made of a '*sublime* material, of that other "indestructible and immutable" body which persists beyond the corruption of the body physical – this other body of money is like the corpse of the Sadeian victim which endures all torments and survives with its beauty immaculate'.

> This immaterial corporeality of the 'body within the body' gives us a precise definition of the sublime object. (SOI 12)

It is not without reason that Marx resorts to the anthropologist's notion of 'fetishism' in his analysis of capital. The fact is that people treat money as religious folk behave around their fetish. It is for them a natural thing endowed with supernatural powers. People are prepared to die for it or do the impossible, as they are for their fetish or their nation or in the name of their 'way of life' and so on – for anything, that is, that strikes them sublime. Why? Because it is invested with the promise of bringing its owner fullness, 'happiness', coincidence of self with self. It's as if its possession guaranteed its owner that her experience of being constantly unsatisfied in life is at an end.

Let's say that I buy a pair of jeans for a 100 dollars. In exchanging the one for the other, the buyer and salesperson mistake the social reality of money for one of its material properties. Both the salesperson and I think that money is inherently a means of exchange, that is, owing to one of its physical properties. Something social is mistaken for something natural, something subjective for something objective. What does the social reality of money consist in? What does value consist in? For Marx, it consists in abstract labour time. Two items have the same value if an equal amount of time is socially necessary to produce them. The value of a thing is determined by the amount of time necessary to bring it about. Now ideology doesn't simply consist in the reification of labour power. The social-immaterial quality of money represents abstract labour time, yes, but labour is the social nature of man and money at bottom represents the symbolic order. What is hypostatized in the exchange of a pair of jeans for money is *society*. What does that mean?

The first thing to say about the symbolic order is that it is a formal structure that behaves a little like Kant's categories and the forms of space and time. They constitute a framework that individuates and renders intelligible what there is. The symbolic order consists of differences, including the differences between the psyche and material nature. It is a chain whose elements (signifiers) are differentially articulated. There are no positive terms in it, terms with an identity and content of their own. All of its terms are determined negatively in their relations with one another. Signifiers are combined with or substituted for one another according to a finite set of rules. These are the two symbolic operations: combination and substitution, metonymy and metaphor, the institution of syntagmatic (lateral) and paradigmatic (vertical) relations. For Žižek and Lacan, the symbolic order is both immaterial *and* contingent. This is less paradoxical than it sounds once we realize that its contingency is a function of its inherent limit. The symbolic order is *constitutively open*. It is absolutely impossible that it should form a closed totality. It is in itself –

that is, ontologically – inconsistent and lacking. It lacks the positive term (the signified) that would put an end to the deferral of meaning and that would close it on itself. The upshot is that not everything that is contingent (i.e. open to variation and change) is for that reason material.[1]

The ideological effect Žižek studies is then the following: a *necessary* (constitutive) *limit* to the possibility of closure, of society being at one and in harmony with itself, becomes, by means of fantasy, an *empirical obstacle* – the other, the social pariah, is posited as an obstacle, as one whose removal will restore the social harmony. Generally speaking, the ideological gesture doesn't simply consist in mistaking a particular and contingent truth for a necessary and universal one. It consists in the opposite gesture as well, in *historically relativizing*, and *seeing as contingent*, a non-contingent, *inherent* or *structural limit*.[2]

Exchange: Alfred Sohn-Rethel

Žižek (SOI 9-16) draws on Alfred Sohn-Rethel's *Intellectual and Manual Labour: A Critique of Epistemology* (1978) (whom he cites in the passages quoted earlier) in order to make two points. The first is that the act of exchange accomplishes an abstraction of the kind presupposed by the modern scientific view of nature. When the scientist studies nature, she doesn't have before her individual animals, trees, rocks and the like in the wealth of their sensory plenitude. She thinks away their sensory properties – what Locke calls 'secondary qualities' – and studies something general and abstract: matter distributed in uniform space and time whose behavior obeys the laws of motion. The same occurs in the act of exchange. The seller and buyer unknowingly abstract the sensory properties from the items they exchange because what matters to them is their worth. Neither of them is aware of the fact that in exchanging goods, they reduce a use value to an exchange value. The point is that exchange would not be possible if they were aware of what they're doing.

> the social effectivity of the exchange process is a kind of reality which is possible only on condition that the individuals partaking in it are *not* aware

> of its proper logic; that is, a kind of reality *whose very ontological consistency implies a certain non-knowledge of its participants* – if we come to 'know too much', to pierce the true functioning of social reality, this reality would dissolve itself. (SOI 15)

The implication – and this is Žižek's second point – is that ideology is not simply false consciousness but, instead, that false consciousness is integral to the functioning of society. The latter depends upon the epistemic state of its members. Society would not be possible except insofar as its members are ignorant of how it works. Inversely, the knowledge of how it works – that is to say, *science* – entails the suspension of capitalist society and its transformation into a free society.

We are here still within the parameters of classical Marxism with its opposition between science and ideology. To enlighten consciousness about the way things are is to put an end to ideology and to transform consciousness into an agent of historical change. Ideology endures so long as the naivety of consciousness endures. And Žižek rightly wonders whether this conception still applies today.

> Does this concept of ideology as a naïve consciousness still apply to today's world? Is it still operating today? (SOI 25)

Cynical consciousness: Peter Sloterdijk

Žižek responds with an unequivocal 'no' in the background of his reading of Peter Sloterdijk's *Critique of Cynical Reason* (1983). I cannot deal with the complexity and wealth of detail of Sloterdijk's *Critique*. I limit myself to his comments on cynicism and leave out his reflections on kynicism.

Sloterdijk's claim in Part 1 of the *Critique* is that the critique of ideology is at an end because cynicism has exhausted its resources. Cynicism is a feature of modern consciousness prominent particularly during the Weimar Republic (1918–1933). Who is the cynic? She is the average educated member of mass industrial society. She is Everyman. She is the kind of person who doesn't want to be fooled or taken for a sucker by what the world throws at her.

> It is the universally widespread way in which enlightened people see to it that they are not taken for suckers. There even seems to be something healthy in this attitude, which, after all, the will to self-preservation generally supports. It is the stance of people who realize that the times of naivety are gone.[3]

The cynic is a member of parliament. She sits on commissions and councils. She works for a publishing company. She is an academic, a lawyer, a doctor, a professional of one sort or another. Educated and with a mind of her own, she sees through the bullshit. She has no faith in the established order. She knows that it is rotten yet she acts as if she doesn't know.

> Cynicism is *enlightened false consciousness*. It is that modernized, unhappy consciousness, on which enlightenment has labored both successfully and in vain. It has learned its lessons in enlightenment, but it has not, and probably was not able to, put them into practice. Well-off and miserable at the same time, this consciousness no longer feels affected by any critique of ideology; its falseness is already reflexively buffered.[4]

Sloterdijk's observation is apt as a description of the contemporary situation. It's not as if consumer culture is unaware of its shallowness. The egregious crime – at least since the 1990s – is naivety, sincerity and conviction.[5] The fear is to be the dupe of the system and pass for a sucker. The default attitude is cynicism, irony, laughter and irreverence. The best car commercials, for instance, are those that mock the car industry. Isn't Trump's presidency American culture's way of making a mockery of its political and moral institutions, its way of exposing their emptiness?

The cynic is a political and moral nihilist. She is aware that society's beliefs and ideals are without substance, that they are mere image, play and deception. The falseness of ideology is 'reflexively buffered'. No one is taken in by them or by such Hollywood clichés as 'If you build it, they will come', that is, that happiness comes to those who work hard or that hard work is its own reward and so on.

> It is clear, therefore, that confronted with such cynical reason, the traditional critique of ideology no longer works. We can no longer subject the ideological text to 'symptomatic reading', confronting it with its blank

> spots, with what it must repress to organize itself, to preserve its consistency – cynical reason takes this distance into account in advance. Is then the only issue left to us to affirm that, with the reign of cynical reason, we find ourselves in the so-called post-ideological world?

'Naivety' and 'critique' are the terms between which the process of enlightenment (understood as a process of education) takes place. Enlightenment is the relentless drive to unmask illusions. Its aim is to raise consciousness out of its state of naivety and dogmatism and make it critically self-aware. The cynic is someone who has undergone this process of enlightenment – the cynic is an enlightened consciousness – yet what makes her position false is the fact that she acts against her better knowledge. She knows that society is ridden with conflicts. Nevertheless, she acts as if she doesn't know and everything is in good order. Why? Because she is motivated by 'the forces of circumstances and the instinct of self-preservation'.

Cynical consciousness shares some features with perversion understood as a clinical category. Lacan distinguishes between the neurotic, the pervert and the psychotic. In his eyes, what differentiates them is their respective relation to the Law, that is, the big Other. Let me say a word about perversion. Lacan thinks of perversion on the basis of fetishism. The different kinds of perversion – sadism, masochism and so on, – are different kinds of fetishism. Its defining feature is the disavowal of castration. Consider the theory of sexuality a 5–7-year-old boy invents when he first takes note of the female anatomy. To begin with, he attributes to everyone a male genital. He thinks that males and females have a penis. He cannot imagine how anyone could be without such a pleasure-giving organ. Let's say his mother is the first woman he sees naked. On seeing her, he imagines that she was castrated, and, naturally, he begins to fear for the loss of his own penis. To this end, he denies – he disavows – his perception of her missing phallus. He pretends that she is not castrated. What is the fetish? It is a memorial of the subject's and of the Other's castration and of its disavowal. It is a substitute for the missing phallus. The pervert (fetishist) is someone who knows that his mother doesn't have a penis and who nonetheless acts as if he doesn't know, as if she still has one.

The same goes for the cynic. The cynic knows that society is ridden with conflicts and inequalities. Nevertheless, he acts as if he doesn't know, as if there is an underlying order and harmony, as if the mother has the phallus. Ideology operates at the level of what he does, not at the level of what he knows.

> the illusion is not on the side of knowledge, it is already on the side of reality itself, of what people are doing. What they do not know is that their social reality itself, their activity, is guided by an illusion, by a fetishistic inversion. (SOI 29-30)

The formula of ideology for the Marxist is 'they don't know it, but they do it anyway'. The worker doesn't know that he is alienating his labour power but he does it anyway. The formula of ideology for Žižek is 'they know it, but they do it anyway'. The cynic knows that society is lacking but he acts as if he doesn't know. Further, 'he acts as if he doesn't know' involves an unconscious mechanism of projection. It involves attributing disavowed beliefs to the big Other.

Belief and ideology

Let me cite the following passage from the section titled 'The objectivity of belief'.

> This is how we should grasp the fundamental Lacanian proposition that psychoanalysis is not a psychology: the most intimate beliefs, even the most intimate emotions such as compassion, crying, sorrow, laughter, can be transferred, delegated to others without losing their sincerity. (SOI 32)

We can distinguish between conscious and unconscious beliefs. Conscious beliefs are, generally speaking, identified as mental states. They function as reasons for belief and action. An unconscious belief is nothing of the sort. It is not a belief you're committed to or you claim as your own. It is, in this instance, disavowed. Or, what amounts to the same thing, it is attributed to the big Other. In that sense, disavowal constitutes the social setting of human interaction. What I say and how I speak to you depend in large measure on what I unconsciously take you to believe.

Consider the Greek chorus in ancient Greek tragedy or the canned laughter of sitcoms. What we take for spontaneous behaviour – for example laughter – is in fact a duty. Moreover, such duties are delegated to others. The spectator comes to the theatre with his worries and everyday problems. He is unable to feel the required fear and pity, 'but no problem, there is the Chorus, who feels the sorrow and the compassion instead of us'. (SOI 32) Canned laugher implies 'the paradox that laughter is a matter of duty and not of some spontaneous feeling' (SOI 33) and that it can be delegated to the big Other.

> What we call 'social reality' is in the last resort an ethical construction; it is supported by a certain *as if* (we act *as if* we believe in the almightiness of bureaucracy, *as if* the President incarnates the Will of the People, *as if* the Party expresses the objective interest of the working class . . .). As soon as the belief [. . .] is lost, the very texture of the social field disintegrates. (SOI 34)

I want to flesh out what is at stake in attributing disavowed beliefs to the big Other. Let me cite the final scene in Chapter 39 of Don DeLillo's *White Noise*. Jack Gladney enters a church bleeding and is shocked to learn that the German nuns there don't believe in God, heaven, hell and the like. They believe in such things for others – that is, for unbelievers and cynics like himself – but not for themselves. They're not fools! the nun insists.

> 'But you're a nun. Nuns believe these things. When we see a nun, it cheers us up, it's cute and amusing, being reminded that someone still believes in angels, in saints, all the traditional things.'
>
> 'You would have a head so dumb to believe this?'
>
> 'It's not what I believe that counts. It's what you believe.'
>
> 'This is true', she said. 'The nonbelievers need the believers. They are desperate to have someone believe. But show me a saint. Give me one hair from the body of a saint.'
>
> She leaned toward me, her stark face framed in the black veil. I began to worry.

'We are here to take care of sick and injured. Only this. You would talk about heaven, you must find another place.'

'Other nuns wear dresses,' I said reasonably. 'Here you still wear the old uniform. The habit, the veil, the clunky shoes. You must believe in tradition. The old heaven and hell, the Latin mass. The Pope is infallible, God created the world in six days. The great old beliefs. Hell is burning lakes, winged demons.'

'You would come in bleeding from the street and tell me six days it took to make a universe?'

'On the seventh He rested.'

'You would talk of angels? Here?'

'Of course here. Where else?'

I was frustrated and puzzled, close to shouting.

'Why not armies that would fight in the sky at the end of the world?'

'Why not? Why are you a nun anyway? Why do you have that picture on the wall?'

She drew back, her eyes filled with contemptuous pleasure.

'It is for others. Not for us.'

'But that's ridiculous. What others?'

'All the others. The others who spend their lives believing that *we* still believe. It is our task in the world to believe things no one else takes seriously. To abandon such beliefs completely, the human race would die. This is why we are here. A tiny minority. To embody old things, old beliefs. The devil, the angels, heaven, hell. If we did not pretend to believe these things, the world would collapse.'[6]

Jack Gladney gets anxious when he hears the nun telling him that she herself doesn't believe in the old ideological claptrap about God, heaven and hell, and that she and the other nuns pretend to believe so that people like him – self-proclaimed atheists and cynics – don't have to. The problem in part is that if she doesn't believe, he will have to become a sincere believer. Put differently, cynicism and ideology aren't incompatible as Sloterdijk suggests. The subject is a cynic by projecting on the big Other beliefs he disavows. 'The big Other believes, not me, the big Other is naïve, not me.' The big Other must be naïve for the cynic. Further, the cynic's position is ideological because *by attributing those beliefs to the big Other, he masks its lack.*

In 'Foreword to the Second Edition' of *For They Know Not What They Do: Enjoyment as a Political Factor* (1991), Žižek distinguishes between the traditional and the modern subject of ideology. Both share the view that the ideological text is not to be taken literally. In other words, neither of them is naïve. They both disidentify with the big Other. But whereas the traditional subject pretends to believe in religious claims – he says he does when he doesn't – the modern subject represses his belief, that is, he attributes it to the big Other; and in that sense, he conceals from himself the fact that the big Other is castrated, that is, lacking.

The nun reveals to Jack Gladney the fact that she is missing the phallus – that she doesn't believe sincerely, that she is as much of a cynic as he is; and since she embodies the big Other, she reveals to him the fact that the big Other is castrated. Whence Gladney's anxiety.

What Sloterdijk misses is the role played by the unconscious in ideology in the sense described. (He otherwise remarks on the critical import, for the history of the enlightenment tradition, of the discovery of the unconscious.) The cynic is enlightened on the surface. There is an unconscious mechanism that keeps him trapped in the ideological understanding of society as a completed totality.

Althusser: Interpellation and misrecognition

For Žižek, ideology is coextensive with the socialization of the human body. It is not surprising, therefore, that psychoanalysis, with its theory of the formation of the unconscious and of the ego during infancy and early childhood, proves to be of critical importance for unmasking its effects. The implication, furthermore, is that ideology and the unconscious coincide. Althusser draws this implication in 'Ideology and Ideological State Apparatuses' (1969). He assimilates ideology to the Freudian unconscious by saying that the one and the other are timeless (he mistakenly writes 'eternal') and without history. Ideology has no history and it can and must 'be related directly to Freud's proposition that the *unconscious is eternal*, i.e., that it has no history'.[7] His intention is not to highlight an interesting comparison. It is to express an identity of essence. Ideology and the unconscious are consubstantial, the unconscious understood in Lacan's sense as a symbolic machine structuring the customs – the rituals and practices – that engage its members.

The crux of Althusser's theory is interpellation and the scene he uses to illustrate it, that is, the transformation of the individual into a subject, is well-known. Someone in the street, a person in authority, a police officer, calls out 'Hey, you!'. I turn round thinking that he's calling me. I recognize myself in his call. The point is that the call never misses its target, 'they hardly ever miss their man'. The individual is interpellated when addressed by the big Other, which takes place prior to birth. The call (the signifier) in the form of the family name, for instance, pre-exists the individual. It determines in advance a plurality of subject-positions.

> verbal call or whistle: the one hailed always recognizes that it is really him who is being hailed. And yet it is a strange phenomenon, and one which cannot be explained solely by 'guilty feelings', despite the large numbers who 'have something on their consciences'.[8]

Guilt has nothing to do with it. It is not why I turn round. Guilt is consequent to the subject's (mis)recognition of himself. I feel guilty for not being Christian enough if I identify as Christian. The superego lashes out on account of the positions the subject occupies in the symbolic network.

Althusser's theory explains the formation of the subject. Given the significance of interpellation (the signifier), it goes without saying that 'the subject' is a linguistic category. It is a matter of names, signifiers and the positions they carve out in reality. The two agents on the scene – the police officer and the man in the street – are figurative representations of, respectively, society and the individual. There is a vertical relation between them. Society dictates the terms under which the individual identifies himself and becomes a subject. Althusser's point is that society constrains the individual to *consent* to the subject-positions he occupies. This is what distinguishes ideological state apparatuses (family, school, church, trade unions, media, the arts, etc.) from state apparatuses (army, police, courts, prison, administration, government, etc.). They operate by way of ideology to manufacture consent. State apparatuses, by contrast, use violence and coercion. Althusser acknowledges that there is a measure of coercion and consent in both ideological and non-ideological state apparatuses. Nevertheless, his point is that one is characteristic of ideological and the other of non-ideological state apparatuses.

Misrecognition is key to the mechanism of interpellation. Society tells the individual 'You are that' – 'You are white, female, unmarried, heterosexual' and so on – and the individual recognizes herself as such. She acknowledges that she is what society says she is, 'Yes, I am that.' At stake is Lacan's mirror stage. The infant sees, in the specular reflection of her body, a unified subject when in fact she experiences herself as a manifold of drives and as utterly helpless and dependent on the caregiver. Though she sees herself in the mirror as an independent and autarchic being, she is dependent on the (m)Other both for the necessities of life and, what is no less necessary, the feeling of being loved or of being worthy of the Other's love. The infant mistakenly takes for her ego the image she sees in the mirror. The same happens with the interpellation of the subject.

Let us imagine that the infant receives an education at home, at school and at church. She has learnt to sing the national anthem and 'Shine Jesus Shine'. She is told to behave like a 'good little girl' and so on. The result? The accidents of her birth – the fact that she was born in this country, in this religion, with this sex and so on – becomes for her the expression of a substantial ego. She takes contingent features for necessary ones. It doesn't help that teachers and parents keep reminding their children who they are, 'you are African', 'you are Christian' and so on, 'and, therefore, you should [or shouldn't] do that'. On the contrary, it is then that ideology kicks in. Once children say 'Yes, I am that' or they acknowledge that they are what they are interpellated as, the accidental properties of their life are transformed, as if by magic, into something quite different. Some of the features of the culture they are born into become for them the defining features of their self. Owing to a retrospective illusion, they come to think that they have always been what they are now.

Žižek takes issue with Althusser on the ground that (mis)recognition doesn't account for the fact that the subject remains wedded to state ideological apparatus (the symbolic order). It can't be out of habit that the subject remains attached to them, for they cause it *jouissance*, that is, pleasure in displeasure. I am not saying that going to school or church and so on is for the subject a matter of *jouissance*, but that the latter results from the subject's submission to the signifier (in the interpellatory process), which is always a violent event. It coincides with a traumatism, with the loss of the Real, that is, castration. Žižek's paradoxical claim is that the subject remains attached to ideological state apparatuses as to a trauma or symptom.

Put differently, Althusser doesn't seem to consider the fact that (mis) recognition – the individual's entrance into society – produces a remainder. The socialization of individuals forms not only subjects, but *symptoms* as well. (Lacan will even define the 'ego' as a symptom.) Now symptoms are pathological disturbances. They are phenomena in the symbolic field that refuse to be integrated. They are symbolically recalcitrant. They are pieces of the Real. Yet they are the very thing that keeps the subject tied to certain discourses, performative utterances, ideological state apparatuses – in short, to the signifier. The subject's relation to language is sustained by a certain traumatism.

Take a common symptom. A man compulsively washes his hands. (Note too that pathological phenomena in general have the feature Freud ascribes to the death drive, that is, the compulsion to repeat. Symptoms are animated by, in part or as a whole, the death drive.) A symptom is a pathological behaviour that causes the patient pain. Generally speaking, Freud describes it as a substitute satisfaction for the drive or one of its representatives, that is, a wish or fantasy whose actualization society prohibits. Let us say that our symptom represents an unconscious masturbatory fantasy, one curtailed in childhood by a parental figure. 'I will cut it off if I see you do it again'. Because the fantasy violates a social norm, the drive finds satisfaction in an asexual substitute, in the ritual washing of hands. A symptom normally comprises several layers that do not always sit well together. The unconscious masturbatory wish is likely to be associated with an unconscious feeling of guilt and repeatedly and intensely washing one's hands could very well serve the dual function of realizing the masturbatory wish and of relieving the guilt by fraying the skin on one's hands to the point of causing oneself pain, that is, as a means of punishment. (The guilt lessens if I unconsciously believe I've been punished for the crime.) It is essential to keep in mind the paradoxical nature of the symptom. The fact is that the patient remains *attached* to a pattern of behaviour that *causes her pain* and that is at odds with her welfare. No amount of talking – of symbolic mediation – can liberate her from it. The symptom may persist even after its sense has been deciphered. What is required is an alteration at the level of the subject's *relation to the Real*, what Žižek calls after Lacan 'traversing the fantasy'.

Žižek's insight is that a subject invests in the state ideological apparatuses in which she is formed in the same way that a patient invests in her symptoms, for that is how the drive procures for itself satisfaction (*jouissance*). The subject's most profoundly unyielding link to the symbolic order (ideology) is pre-symbolic. After all, isn't ideology at bottom a pathological disorder and symptom?

Consider the husband who suspects his wife of cheating on him. Let us say that he is right. His wife cheats on him all the time. That doesn't change the fact that his jealousy is a paranoid construction.

> even if all the facts he quotes in support of his jealousy are true, even if his wife really is sleeping around with other men, this does not change one bit the fact that his jealousy is a pathological, paranoid construction. (SOI 49)

Naturally the same is true of the anti-Semitic figure of the Jew, of the racist image of blacks, of the xenophobic image of the foreigner and so on. Even if what the anti-Semite says about Jews is true (e.g. that they exploit the population and seduce young Christian girls, etc.), it doesn't change the fact that his hatred is pathological. His figure of the Jew doesn't denote an actual ethnic group. It is a response to a proliferating multiplicity of questions, 'Why am I being exploited?', 'Why are the traditional beliefs fading?', 'Why am I not finding a job?' and so on. It offers the anti-Semite an unequivocal answer to these anxiety-provoking questions and it restores a measure of stability to the social field. The figure of the Jew is a fantasy in which he invests in order to be rescued from the appalling realization that the big Other is ontologically inconsistent and lacking. It proffers up the promise of harmony by identifying the (supposed) cause of disharmony (i.e. the Jew). It masks the gap in the big Other. Althusser misses this crucial role played by fantasy in ideology.

For Althusser, the subject comes into existence as a result of an act of identification or, what amounts to the same thing, of (mis)recognition, 'Yes, that's who I am.' For psychoanalysis, the subject of the unconscious comes into existence as a result of an act of *dis*identification, 'No, that's not who I am. I don't dispute that I compulsively wash my hands, but I do *not* recognize myself in that gesture.' The symptom resists symbolization-understanding-meaning. It causes interpellation to fail. It is, paradoxically, both the inherent limit of the symbolic order and the positive condition of its existence. For what is at stake, after all, is the traumatism of the body's immemorial and inaugural subjection to the signifier. I take it that this is what Žižek is getting at in this difficult passage.

> this external 'machine' of State Apparatuses exercises its force only in so far as it is experienced, in the unconscious economy of the subject, as a traumatic, senseless injunction. Althusser speaks only of the process of ideological interpellation through which the symbolic machine of ideology is 'internalized' into the ideological experience of Meaning and Truth: but we can learn from Pascal that this 'internalization', by structural necessity, never fully succeeds, that there is always a residue, a leftover, a stain of traumatic irrationality and senselessness sticking to it, and that *this leftover, far from hindering the full submission of the subject to the ideological command, is the very condition of it*: it is precisely this non-integrated surplus of senseless traumatism which confers on the Law its unconditional authority: in other words, which – in so far as it escapes ideological sense – sustains what we might call the ideological *jouis-sense*, enjoyment-in-sense (enjoy-meant), proper to ideology. (SOI 43)

Ideological state apparatuses – customs with their rituals, practices and rules – consist of a network of signifiers that is lacking, 'castrated'. The lack (of sense, of a signified) in the big Other is the cause of the subject's *dis*identification. It is why the subject wonders whether she really is what society (the big Other) says she is. It is why Žižek accords hysteria an ontological and political priority (see the following). Here Žižek seems to be saying that the body's senseless subjection to the signifier confers on the latter its unqualified authority. The idea seems to be that the authority of a law, of a word passed or issued as law, is all the greater, is unconditional, the more incomprehensible it is or the more incomprehensible the lawgiver's reason for it is. The unconditional authority of the moral law in Kant, for instance, coincides with its incomprehensibility to the finite human mind. Let me in effect explain what I take Žižek to be getting at from the point of view of the Kantian notion of the Law he is here introducing.

Kant and the Law

In Žižek's discourse if not also in Lacan's, 'Law' (capitalized) is a term that refers either to the social order or to the Freudian drive, that is, the Symbolic or the Real. In the former instance, it evokes in Lacan the Name-of-the-Father whose appearance, in the life of the subject, signals the resolution of the Oedipal complex. It is a signifier whose function is to draw limits, boundaries, divisions and articulate differences. It separates the child from the mother and furnishes him with a space of his own, a space where he can cease to identify with the object of her desire (the imaginary phallus) and articulate his own in relation to the desire of the big Other. The Law signifies a 'No' to the mother and child. To the mother, 'No, the child is not your phallus; he is not what you're missing.' To the child, 'No, you do not have what she wants (i.e. the phallus).' Lacan explains this in detail in Seminar five *Formations of the Unconscious.*

The term also evokes the categorical imperative in Kant's moral doctrine. The categorical imperative imposes a limit on the subject's self-love. By 'self-love' we should understand broadly the subject's attachment to its sensuous life and its goods, to 'happiness' in the standard pragmatic sense where it names the subject's welfare or the welfare of its own or of those with whom it identifies. Why ought I not to kill, lie, covet another man's wife, and so on? Not because it causes others harm, but because it is intrinsically wrong. If fulfilling my moral duty costs me my life, then so be it. For Kant, the authority of the moral Law is absolute, indivisible, infinite and so on. There is from this angle a kinship between the Law and the Freudian drive. They are both 'ethical' in the special sense Žižek reserves for acts transformative of the symbolic coordinates of the established order. The sense in which an act is 'ethical' is the extent to which it suspends the pleasure and reality principles or, what amounts to the same thing in this context, the living being's homeostatic balance and adaptation to the pressure of environmental forces. An act is 'ethical' provided it issues from the drive or Law – that is, provided the agency constraining the will commands it *unconditionally*, that is, regardless of the consequences for the welfare of living beings. Put differently, *attachment to the Law coincides with a readiness to die*. It is an attachment to nothingness or a detachment from life and its goods. Žižek often cites as an example Antigone in Sophocles' eponymous play. She defies the law of the city that prohibits the burial of its enemies. She knowingly goes to her death by burying her slain brother. She responds to an unconditional imperative.

What exerts itself on the subject with unconditional force or as an unconditional obligation – that is, the Law or drive – is beyond finite, human knowledge. Kafka's *The Trial* is usually cited to exemplify the fact. K is accused of a crime. He is not told of what crime and the authority accusing him is inaccessible. The Law is an exteriority at the heart of the subject. The subject's most intimate interiority is more *foreign* to it than the exteriority of space and material nature. Lacan's term for this experience of the Freudian drive in Seminar seven *The Ethics of Psychoanalysis* is 'extimacy'. The Law commands absolutely, not because it is good or wise or just, predicates that are derivative, conditional and empirical in character. It is 'the moral law that first determines and makes possible the concept of the good, insofar as it deserves this name absolutely'.[9] The Law commands absolutely *because it is the Law*. Anything unconditional is without or beyond justification – or, as it is also put, is self-justifying, self-authenticating – and invariably results in such tautologies.

> It follows, from this constitutively senseless character of the Law, that we must obey it not because it is just, good or even beneficial, but simply

> because it is the law – this tautology articulates the vicious circle of its authority, the fact that the last foundation of the Law's authority lies in its process of enunciation. (SOI 35)

The Law (the Real) isn't something other than the symbolic order. It is its constitutive limit. It is because of the Law that the symbolic order is ontologically inconsistent.

In the cited passage, Žižek is saying that the symbolic order isn't self-founding. It rests on speech acts and on the performance of rituals by social actors in the relevant circumstances. That is why the elements and rules of a symbolic structure are always changing. Think of Judith Butler's notion that gender identity isn't fixed somewhere – in the mind or body of a person – and that it is a function of what someone does. To the extent that my gender identity is something I perform, it changes all the time. 'Performance' should be understood here in the broad Derridean sense of repetition, citation, imitation, parody and so on. It doesn't reproduce the same. It produces differences. Now that is not the Lacanian Real. The Real is a difference that traumatizes because it is extra-conceptual, it cannot be signified, its blow cannot be cushioned. It is irreducible to the oppositional differences of the symbolic order (i.e. signifiers). It is a 'meta-difference' or, as Žižek puts it after Laclau and Mouffe, an 'antagonism'. Now the Law is a meta-difference of this kind. It is the senseless unconditional injunction 'Don't!'. Lacking a signifier or, as Kant might put it, content, it limits the symbolic order from within. The Real is why the symbolic order cannot constitute itself as a closed totality.

A 'noble lie' (Plato) is thus invented: 'the Law is not a senseless injunction; far from it, it is the decree of wisdom, of truth, etc.'. A constitutive limit to self-coincidence is turned upside down and made to appear as an external or contingent one. The traumatism of the Real (the presence of lack) is obfuscated by the fantasy – by the promise – of imminent fullness.

> Ideology is not a dreamlike illusion that we build to escape insupportable reality; in its basic dimension it is a fantasy-construction which serves as a support for our 'reality' itself: an 'illusion' which structures our effective,

real social relations and thereby masks some insupportable, real, impossible kernel [. . .] The function of ideology is not to offer us a point of escape from our reality but to offer us the social reality itself as an escape from some traumatic, real kernel. (SOI 45)

Note Žižek's two claims here:

- Ideology rests on the signifier and fantasy. It rests on the symbolic order and the Real (i.e. the symptom as the locus of the drive's *jouissance*).
- Ideology-cum-fantasy isn't a distortion of social reality. It distorts the traumatic Real. How? By causing the subject to believe that it is self-transparent and autonomous and that it exits in a closed world.

Disidentification

Let me add a final point in conclusion. It concerns Žižek's criticism of Althusser. He makes the point clearly in his first contribution to *Contingency, Hegemony, Universality: Contemporary Dialogues on the Left* (2000).

the subject emerges only when and in so far as interpellation liminally *fails*. Not only does the subject never fully recognize itself in the interpellative call: its resistance to interpellation (to the symbolic identity provided by interpellation) *is* the subject. In psychoanalytic terms, this failure of interpellation is what *hysteria* is about; for this reason, the subject *as such* is, in a way, hysterical. That is to say: what is hysteria if not the stance of the permanent questioning of one's symbolic identity, of the identity conferred on me by the big Other: 'You say I am (a mother, a whore, a teacher . . .), but *am I really what you say I am?* What is in me that makes me what you say I am?' (CHU115)

Interpellation fails on account of the symptom, that is, the Real, that is, the gap between the subject and the symbolic machine. Žižek explains three different things with this.

- The subject's *non-symbolic attachment* to the symbolic order, that is, through *jouissance* and trauma.
- The subject is '*as such*' hysterical. This quasi-ontological assertion says that *disidentification* is *the constitutive mode of being of the subject*. Why is it '*as such*' hysterical? Presumably because it is exposed to the lack in the big Other that causes it to question whether it is what the big Other says it is.
- The ontological pre-eminence Žižek grants hysteria must be understood against the common gesture, in political theories on the left, of privileging perversion. The common wisdom is that the pervert is a progressive type. He breaks with social and moral taboos and unmasks their arbitrariness. The cross-dresser, the homosexual, and so on, make conspicuous the contingency (the non-necessity) of heterosexual normativity. Žižek departs from this common wisdom for various reasons. In the first place, irreverence, laughter, irony, parody, cynicism and so on are part of the reigning ideology. Everybody knows that social and moral taboos are not to be taken seriously, or rather, everybody knows that one is expected to behave *as if* they were absolutely authoritative. In the second place, the practice of violating taboos is the obscene underside of the official Law or public face of the party. Žižek develops this insight in several places. He covers it at length in Chapter 3 of *The Metastases of Enjoyment: Six Essays on Woman and Causality*. The idea is twofold. On the one hand, it is that the *superego* enjoining the subject to transgress the rules and take pleasure in it *appears whenever the Law fails*. The superego is to the Law what the primal father of the primal horde in Freud's *Totem and Taboo* – the pre-castrated father ruthlessly enjoying the women he owns – is to the symbolic father, that is, the signifier with which the subject identifies at the end of the Oedipal drama. The superego is cruel. It enjoins transgression and excess. The symbolic father is the Law that councils restraint and moderation. Žižek's observation is that the superego emerges whenever the symbolic father and, correlatively, the Oedipal organization of the subject are in decline. On the other hand, transgression is the very thing

> that keeps a community together. A subject who meticulously follows its explicit rules is not accepted by its members as 'one of us' so long as she does not participate in the transgressive rituals 'which actually keep this community together'. (NEP lxi) A community is held together by identifying with its specific form of transgression. Žižek provides numerous examples of this, including 'the nightly terror of Ku Klux Klan, with its lynchings of powerless blacks' (CHU 55), 'code red' in Rob Reiner's *A Few Good Men*, Nazi pogroms like Kristallnacht, and so on. What are the *political consequences* of this? Žižek is clear about them in his second contribution in *Contingency, Hegemony, Universality: Contemporary Dialogues on the Left*.

> in so far as power relies on its 'inherent transgression', then – sometimes, at least – *overidentifying* with the explicit power discourse – *ignoring* this inherent obscene underside and simply taking the power discourse at its (public) word, acting as if it really means what it explicitly says (and promises) – can be the most effective way of disturbing its smooth functioning. (CHU 220)

Not disidentification then, but overidentification can sometimes subvert the existing order. If power doesn't expect you to take what it says seriously or at its word, then you are bound to destabilize it by taking it seriously or at its word.

Study questions

1. How does Žižek respond to Sloterdijk's claim that cynicism has exhausted the resources of the critique of ideology?
2. What are Žižek's criticisms of Althusser?

Section 2

We can understand the link between Chapters 1 and 2 of *The Sublime Object of Ideology* as follows. The overall aim of Chapter 2 is to spell out in detail the concluding insights of Chapter 1 where Žižek highlights the importance of fantasy and the drive (*jouissance*) in attaching the subject to ideology. He argues at the end of Chapter 2 that what matters in an ideology is less its content than its form. By its form, he means the constraint it exercises on the subject to renounce pleasures. This renunciation produces a surplus-enjoyment (*jouissance*) – a satisfaction at the level of the drive – that weds the subject to ideology. The 'real aim of ideology is the attitude demanded by it'. (SOI 90)

The use of the indefinite article – 'an' ideology – is, however, misleading. Žižek doesn't have in mind a superstructural phenomenon like a political doctrine or religion. 'Ideology' denotes the processes of subjectivation taking place in the home, the school, the church and so on, along with the enjoyment (*jouissance*) obtained by the drive through their means. Although Žižek uses the term in various ways, the Lacanian sense he insists on mostly in *The Sublime Object of Ideology* and in works published thereafter is the belief in the existence of the big Other – in other words, the idea that society is a totality. The Right as much as the Left is prey to ideology in that sense. It does not matter how society is conceived, whether as an organic totality where the parts are internally connected to each other and they are subservient to the aims of the whole, or as a formal contract between atomized individuals where each pursues his or her self-interest and there is a sovereign figure (the State) that protects their freedoms and rights. The big Other is presumed to exist in both cases. It is presumed to exist as an already realized totality or as one that is yet to be realized (by, for instance, removing what are taken to be external obstacles to its self-coincidence and harmony). What is occluded in both cases is the deadlock of the Real of the drive.

Žižek is concerned in Chapter 2 with laying out the paradoxes of a symptom. His main interlocutors in Chapters 1 and 2 – Althusser, Laclau and Mouffe – do not, for one reason or another, show the importance, in the critique of ideology, of the place of the symptom, that is, of the drive's enjoyment (*jouissance*). It is for this reason that both chapters belong together as Part I under the heading 'The Symptom'.

Retroactivity (*Nachträglichkeit*)

Let me start with the temporal paradox of the symptom's meaning. Žižek says that it comes from the future. How is that to be understood?

> The Lacanian answer to the question 'From where does the repressed return?' is therefore, paradoxically, 'From the future.' Symptoms are meaningless traces, their meaning is not discovered, excavated from the hidden depth of the past, but constructed retroactively – the analysis produces the truth; that is, the signifying frame which gives the symptoms their symbolic place and meaning. As soon as we enter the symbolic order, the past is always present in the form of historical tradition and the meaning of these traces is not given; it changes continually with the transformations of the signifier's network. Every historical rupture, every advent of a new master-signifier, changes retroactively the meaning of all tradition, restructures the narration of the past, makes it readable in another, new way. (SOI 58)

Let us recall what a symptom is (in addition to the fact that it is described by Freud and Lacan as the 'return of the repressed'). What is involved in the psychoanalytic notion of symptom? It is a *compulsive* behaviour, something irrational and without purpose like a nervous tick which, depending on the symptom, can be detrimental to the agent's welfare, and it has no apparent somatic cause. A symptom is the physical manifestation of an underlying psychical condition (a repressed idea or signifier, a trauma) not accessible to the patient. It is a behaviour pattern that deviates from so-called normality on account of its compulsive character. The paradox Žižek highlights is that a symptom is a signifier (a 'meaningless trace') that precedes in time the meaning (the signified) deciphered in it and that is usually posited as its cause. It is as if, in the case of symptoms, the effect precedes the cause in time. We do not first have the repression and then the return of the repressed. Instead, the return of the repressed is first, whereas its cause or meaning appears later. It is constituted retroactively. 'Retroactivity' is Žižek's translation of Freud's *Nachträglichkeit*, usually rendered 'afterwardsness' or 'delay'.

Let us look at the paradox from a different angle. According to Freud, a symptom is the substitute satisfaction of a repressed wish or fantasy. An unconscious or infantile wish – say, the oral wish for the breast, that is, the wish to be loved, nourished, taken care of by the maternal Other; the anal wish to control bowel movement, that is, the wish to assert one's autonomy and so on – seeks to gain entrance into the consciousness of the adult. It is pushed back. It is forbidden entry. The wish finds an alternative outlet, that is the symptom. For example, the cough or nervous tick is how the wish obtains (illicit) satisfaction. Now Freud claimed early on, in his and Josef Breuer's *Studies on Hysteria* (1895), that it is by verbalizing the unconscious wish, that is, by raising it to the level of consciousness, that the patient can free herself from its compulsive character. He abandoned this view when he realized, in *Beyond the Pleasure Principle* (1920), that compulsive behaviour is a manifestation of the id (the death drive with its compulsion to repeat) and not of a fantasy or wish formed by the system consciousness-preconscious. In other words, analysis is interminable. You cannot liberate yourself from the id or from its ways of finding enjoyment (*jouissance*), but you can learn to live with them in such a way that they don't cause you suffering.

The same is true of the later Lacan. A symptom in Lacan's thought in the early 1950s (the early Lacan) is a coded message addressed to the big Other who is presumed to know its meaning. It arises as a result of a failure of communication, the clogging up of the subject's discourse. The coded message articulates the repressed word and the aim of analysis is to re-establish communication by allowing 'the patient to verbalize the meaning of his symptom: through this verbalization, the symptom is automatically dissolved' (SOI 79). Yet the fact is that the symptom often persists after it has been interpreted. Why does it not dissolve? Because it is not simply a coded message. It is how the subject organizes his enjoyment; 'that is why, even after the completed interpretation, the subject is not prepared to renounce his symptom' (SOI 80). We must distinguish between the symptom's symbolic dimension and its Real one. A symptom is a message addressed to the big Other and it is a particular way in which the subject organizes her enjoyment.

Lacan introduces the notion of sinthome in Seminar twenty-three *The Sinthome* to broach this issue. A symptom understood as a sinthome is a signifier whose signifying function is abolished. It doesn't represent anything. It is a signifying formation that has become the site of the subject's enjoyment, that is, the site where the drive is objectified as a mute, insistent and incomprehensible presence. It is a signifier raised to the level of the Real.[1] Žižek's point is that a symptom remains deprived of meaning until the analyst provides it with a symbolic framework. A symptom is a compulsive disorder whose meaning is constructed by the analyst after the fact.

> the analysis produces the truth; that is, the signifying frame which gives the symptoms their symbolic place and meaning. (SOI 58)

The symptom's meaning doesn't pre-exist, in a state of latency, the symbolic setting in which it is interpreted. It is created by the interpretation. How is this to be understood? Doesn't the repressed wish (the meaning or cause) come before the symptom? What other reason could Freud have had for calling it a 'substitute satisfaction'?

To make sense of this paradox, it is worth emphasizing psychoanalysis' temporal idealism, its claim that there is no objective or value-neutral standpoint from which it is possible to distinguish between the past and the future. This isn't a difference that exists in the nature of things. It is, like every other difference, a function of the symbolic order. Moreover, Freud says in *Beyond the Pleasure Principle* that time as ordered succession is a means devised by the living being to protect itself from the onslaught of excessive stimuli. The conditions of knowledge have a pragmatic value. They are instruments of the reality principle. They are in the service of the adaptation of the living being to the conditions of its social existence. Adaptation is facilitated by being able to plot down stimuli in a common and universally shared temporal framework.

Time doesn't exist in the unconscious. The unconscious doesn't know of the linear chain of causes and effects the conscious mind is habituated to. That is why an unconscious trauma is chronologically unlocalizable. It brings up all sorts of paradoxes, the very paradoxes that we find in the philosophy of time and in science fiction, and it explains why Žižek is preoccupied with science fiction in the chapter.

A traumatic symptom has a non-linear development. It usually involves at least two scenes. Take the case of Emma in Freud's *Project for A Scientific Psychology* (1895). Emma suffers from the compulsion of being unable to enter shops alone. Scene one: Emma at age eight enters a shop and is sexually assaulted by the shopkeeper. He grabs her genitals under her dress. Scene two: Emma at twelve enters a shop and notices that the two shop-assistants are laughing together. She thinks they're laughing at her or at her dress. That triggers her compulsive disorder. Where are we to situate the cause of her trauma? It does not lie in Scene one: at age eight, she was too young to understand that she had been sexually assaulted; there is no evidence that what she experienced then was too much for her, that is, traumatic. It does not lie in Scene two: the shop-assistants didn't assault her sexually. Where then does the trauma come from? It results from the *remembrance* of Scene one *after she reached puberty* and acquired an understanding of (her) sexuality: the memory of Scene one remained latent and started to act pathogenically, like an internal foreign body attacking hers, after puberty set in and in connection with Scene two, which was its occasioning cause: the laughter of the two shop-assistants reminded her of the grin of the shopkeeper who assaulted her. In short, it is mistaken to think of the development of a trauma in linear terms as the effect following its cause in time. A trauma is characterized by a latency period, that is, an irreducible delay, and, most importantly, its cause is internal: it is *not* the event itself but its memory, that is, its *recurrence* and associations with other events, that brings it about.

What is true of the development of a traumatic symptom is true of the constitution of the meaning of a sentence, too. I am thinking of Lacan's claim that retroactivity (*Nachträglichkeit*) is how its meaning is produced. Take the 'elementary cell' in the first version of the graph of desire in 'The Subversion of the Subject and the Dialectic of Desire' (1961) (see Figure 3.2.1).

Graph I

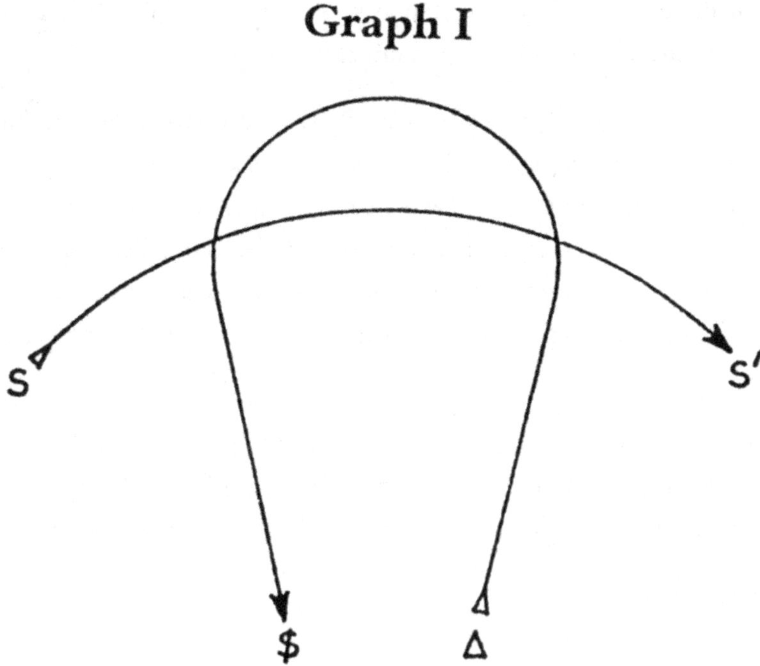

Figure 3.2.1 *The graph of desire, as published in Lacan's essay 'The Subversion of the Subject and the Dialectic of Desire in the Freudian Unconscious', 1960,*

The delta symbol at the bottom right represents the mythical subject of biological need prior to its entry into language ('mythical' because the subject is, even before birth, already subjected to the signifier through, say, the parents' discourse about him or her). The barred S represents the subject split, on account of its submission to language, into the subject of the statement and the subject of enunciation – into what the subject can be conscious of at the level of what it says and the act of enunciation (the emission of signifiers) that eludes consciousness (inasmuch as, in talking, the subject says more than what it means or intends to say): the signifier institutes the difference between consciousness and the unconscious. The vector S-S represents the endless chain of signifiers that is temporarily arrested by a master signifier or *point de capiton*. (More on this later on.) The first version of the graph of desire represents how the subject is caught in the chain of signifiers and how, as a result, it becomes a barred subject, a subject of the unconscious. We might think of the graph as a representation of the immemorial entrance of the subject into society through the medium of language.

> In it [i.e., the elementary cell] is articulated what I have called the 'button tie' (*point de capiton*), by which the signifier stops the otherwise indefinite sliding of signification. [. . .] The diachronic function of this button tie can be found in a sentence, insofar as a sentence closes its signification only with its last term, each term being anticipated in the construction constituted by the other terms and, inversely, sealing their meaning by its retroactive effect.[2]

Lacan's point is fairly straightforward. The meaning of a sentence isn't fixed until its very last word is uttered or written down – until the full stop is marked or signified in some way. If I was to complete the part of the sentence

- I am hungry

with

- for love.

something quite different would be meant than if I was to complete it with

- for nachos.

The meaning of the earlier parts changes with the parts that are added at the end. Meaning doesn't pre-exist language in the thoughts and intentions of speakers. It is the effect of the last word. Lacan's larger point is that the last word – the master signifier – is always an arbitrary one. It is one among many that is selected and set up as the signifier around which the others gravitate and produce a meaning-effect. Looking at it from a historical perspective where the earlier parts of a sentence correspond to the past, we can say that the future holds the key to what occurred in the past, or again, that every time something new happens, the meaning of the entire past changes.

> Every historical rupture, every advent of a new master-signifier, changes retroactively the meaning of all tradition, restructures the narration of the past, makes it readable in another, new way. (SOI 58)

We can understand from this perspective why the meaning of a symptom is determined by the future. A symptom is, like the past, in itself a meaningless trace, a signifier without signified. What happens *next* determines its meaning and how it is to be understood – insofar as what happens next is passed off as the final word on the matter, as, in other words, a master signifier.

Error as the way to the truth

Transference is one of the principal effects of the discourse between the analyst and the analysand. The analysand unconsciously identifies her analyst with, say, her father. This allows the unconscious wishes she may have in relation to her father to appear in the discourse with her analyst in such a way that she can 'work through' them.

According to Lacan, the analysand unconsciously attributes to her analyst a knowledge that he doesn't in fact possess. He is someone who she supposes has the knowledge of the meaning of her symptom. Now this is important because it is the very ideological supposition that the subject has with regards to the big Other. If the big Other knows who or what I am, isn't that because the big Other is in itself complete and consistent, a closed totality lacking nothing? We can see why Žižek assimilates the goal of the critique of ideology to that of analysis. The goal is almost the same. It is to dissolve the subject's fantasy masking the lack in the big Other.

Žižek's point is that the subject's supposition that the big Other knows is a necessary illusion – it is necessary in order to arrive at the meaning of her symptom. It

> is an illusion, it does not really exist in the other, the other does not really possess it, it is constituted afterwards, through our – the subject's – signifier's working; but it is at the same time a *necessary illusion* [my emphasis], because we can paradoxically elaborate this knowledge only by means of the illusion that the other already possesses it and that we are only discovering it. (SOI 58)

The patient mistakenly attributes to her analyst a knowledge he doesn't have. Yet this attribution is necessary to construct this very knowledge and arrive at the meaning of her symptom.

> The transference is an essential illusion by means of which the final Truth (the meaning of a symptom) is produced. (SOI 62)

In the transference, the analyst occupies the position of the subject presumed to know the secret meaning of the patient's desire. The truth at which the patient arrives at the end of analysis is that it is her desire that introduces, in the big Other, the thing that fascinates her about him – notably, the fantasy or *objet a*. Žižek follows Lacan in calling this procedure 'traversing the fantasy'. The larger point Žižek insists on throughout the chapter is that error, or, more precisely, illusion, is the way to the truth. He doesn't doubt that 'the final Truth (the meaning of a symptom)' can be discovered by means of analysis. As with Hegel's dialectic, his claim is that the road to it is paved with errors and illusions. The greatest part of the chapter consists in variations on this theme. The illusion produced by the transference – that the big Other knows the meaning of the subject's symptom – is the first. The variation I want to briefly touch on is what he calls Hegel's 'theory of repetition' (SOI 63) in the *Lectures on the Philosophy of History*. What I said earlier about trauma is here significant. It is not the sexual assault itself that has a pathogenic effect but its remembrance or recurrence at a later date in association with one or more events.

Žižek talks here about the action that Caesar took against Pompey in crossing the Rubicon on the 10 January in 49 BC. It led to civil war and the dissolution of the Roman Republic. Following Hegel, Žižek claims that Caesar's action was in accordance with historical necessity. Caesar clearly saw that the only way to save the unity of the Roman state was to dissolve its Republican form and transform it into an Empire. In the opinion of the people, however, Caesar's action appeared arbitrary. It seemed to them to be the expression of an individual's lust for power. They believed that by removing Caesar, the Republic would regain its splendour. But it was precisely the conspirators against Caesar who revealed the truth in its historical necessity: the outcome of Caesar's murder was the reign of Augustus, the first caesar.

> The Truth thus arose from failure itself: in failing, in missing its express goal, the murder of Caesar fulfilled the task which was, in Machiavellian way, assigned to it by history. (SOI 64)

In failing to restore the Republic through Caesar's murder, the people gave birth to the Roman Empire. They didn't understand Caesar's action. In their attempt to do away with its consequences, they inadvertently repeated it, and it is then that his action struck them in the fullness of its necessity and meaning. What motivated the repetition? The people's perception that Caesar's action was arbitrary and that its consequences could be undone and that the Republican form of government could be restored. On being repeated, however, Caesar's action found a place in the symbolic framework and its meaning was understood. Repetition 'is the way historical necessity asserts itself in the eyes of "opinion"'. (SOI 64)

The other variation on the theme that error is the way to the truth follows on from this one and is, in fact, related to it. It is Freud's account of the parricide in *Totem and Taboo*. Once again, we have here a story about humanity's immemorial entrance into society from the state of nature. The murder of the father and the ensuing guilt leading to the institution of the law (the prohibition against murder and incest, the founding taboos of social coexistence) are the instruments that Freud uses in order to account for this transition. It goes without saying that Freud's story is not to be taken literally. It is best read as a 'fundamental fantasy', that is, as a fantasy of the same kind as the second fantasy in Freud's 'A Child is Being Beaten' (1919). In the first fantasy, the patient imagines her father beating a child she hates. In the second, she imagines herself being beaten by her father. In the third, the patient is the spectator viewing someone beating someone else. The first and third are fantasies the patient recalls having. The second is a construct of analysis used by Freud to explain the first and third yet it is also the Real disavowed by the subject. The second fantasy 'my father is beating me' is how the subject at the same time gratifies her incestuous wish for her father and punishes herself for it. The murder of the primal father and the subsequent guilt instating his law should be read this way, too. It is a construct of analysis and the Real disavowed by the subject. The story is the following. The father of the primal horde is in possession of the women of the tribe. He keeps jealous watch over them and casts out or kills new-born male children. The surviving sons band together and kill him. But instead of enjoying the women, or instead of one of them setting himself up as the successor primal father, the guilt they feel for their crime causes them to institute his law: no one ought to enjoy the women and murder should be prohibited. The father's word does not become an unconditional law while he is alive. It becomes Law, that is, an unconditional constraint on the will of the members of the tribe, upon his death. The sons think that they can overturn his prohibitions by killing him. But it is by killing him that his prohibitions are first instituted. Repetition brings out the necessity and meaning of the father's word. The sons have to first misrecognize what it means. They have to see it as the arbitrary word or action of an individual lusting for power in order to acquire, subsequently, the right understanding of its necessity and significance.

> In other words, the repetition announces the advent of the Law, of the Name-of-the-Father in place of the dead, assassinated father: the event which repeats itself receives its law retroactively, through repetition. (SOI 65)

Žižek's Hegelian point is the following. The sons misrecognize their father's word or action, they take it for something arbitrary just as the people take Caesar's action for something arbitrary. The deficiency they recognize in him is, however, an objectification of their own distorted point of view. The falsity of their position is projected on the other – on Caesar or the primal father. But they recognize that in the repetition or transference. The point is that the distortion of their point of view is not something they can dispense with. They have to pass through the illusion – that the big Other is in itself complete, that Caesar's action is arbitrary and so on – in order to arrive at the truth.

> only the 'working-through' of the misrecognition allows us to accede to the true nature of the other and at the same time overcome our own deficiency. (SOI 67)

The truth cannot arise except through misrecognition. The end of the analytic cure involves

(a) the dissolution of transference, and

(b) 'traversing the fantasy'.

With regards to (a), the analyst no longer occupies the position of the patient's unconscious desire. With regards to (b), the patient sees the *objet a* for what it is – as, notably, a fantasy that plugs up the hole in the big Other as well as in his (the patient's) desire; 'in "going through the fantasy" we experience how this fantasy-object (the "secret") only materializes the void of our desire'. (SOI 69)

The implication Žižek draws from this is that the knowledge produced in analysis can be lethal for the subject. It deprives it of the thing that makes its being consistent, I mean the drive's enjoyment (*jouissance*). Stripped of its 'fundamental fantasy', the subject's being is as it were volatilized. If ignorance is a condition of the drive's enjoyment, then knowing one's desire has the effect of dissolving the *objet a* that causes enjoyment.

> to abolish the misrecognition means at the same time to abolish, to dissolve, the 'substance' which was supposed to hide itself behind the form-illusion of misrecognition. This 'substance' – the only one recognized in psychoanalysis – is, according to Lacan, enjoyment (*jouissance*): access to knowledge is then paid with the loss of enjoyment – enjoyment, in its stupidity, is possible only on the basis of certain non-knowledge, ignorance. (SOI 73)

This is why the analysand's reaction to the analyst is often paranoid. By leading her to know her desire, it's as if he wants to deprive her of the substance of her enjoyment.

Desire and lack

It might be useful at this point to say a word about desire by way of clarifying some of what I have said earlier and what I intend to say further on. Lacan defines desire in 'The Signification of the Phallus' (1958) as 'the difference that results from the subtraction' of need from demand.[3] The formula is: Need – Demand = Desire. By 'need' we are to understand physiological phenomena like thirst or hunger. A demand is a linguistically articulated need. It is the human organism – that is, its biology and physiology – penetrated by the signifier. This rejoins the theme broached twice now regarding the human being's departure from the state of nature. The transition from need to demand coincides with the human being's entrance into society. In this transition (which has never taken place except in immemorial, mythical times), the subject's orientation shifts from the objects that satisfy his needs to the (m)Other that provides him with the objects satisfying his needs. The point Lacan is making is that entrance into society presupposes, as its necessary condition of possibility, the 'space of reason', intersubjectivity, a chain of signifiers. A need aims at an object. It aims at what satisfies it. A demand is aimed at another subject. It is a qualitatively different kind of thing. The linguistic articulation of needs produces something other than a need. What the subject demands of the (m)Other is love, recognition. He wants the (m)Other's unconditional love. That is why the subject is left unsatisfied by the objects he receives from her. It is not because they don't satisfy him. It is because they are for the subject proofs of love, and no matter how many proofs he receives, at bottom they are not what the subject demands. The subject demands not proofs of love but her love, the thing itself, the substance of the (m)Other's enjoyment that, naturally, she cannot give. As Lacan famously puts it in Seminar eight *Transference* and elsewhere, to love is to give someone what you do not have. What you cannot give is your lack or desire. What remains, then, when you subtract need from demand? Nothing at all – that is to say, this lack or void in the subject that is his desire.

Why is the subject plagued by this negativity? Lacan accounts for it in various ways. Let me focus here on his notion of the forced choice in Seminar eleven *The Four Fundamental Concepts of Psychoanalysis*. Lacan thinks that the subject's entrance into society depends on a forced choice, on the same kind of choice the street mugger visits upon his victim: 'Your money or your life?' If you choose your money, you lose both your money and your life. If you choose your life, you lose your money. The point is that you are not given a real choice. Either you lose big or you lose small. In both cases, you lose something. To enter society is to sacrifice a part of yourself. It is to give up something. In truth, of course, one doesn't give up anything. Socialization from infancy onwards has the effect of bringing about a sense that something is lacking in one's life. One goes through life feeling that something is missing, something one cannot quite put one's finger on. Human life revolves around filling this lack. It consists of going through the experience of being unsatisfied by the next best thing or lover or friend that comes to fill it. One loses nothing on entering society but the feeling that something is missing goes on haunting us until the very end. It is an illusion that one cannot simply do away with. It marks the human condition.

The point I want to insist on is that society demands of its members to freely choose what is given to them anyway. I have not chosen the country I was born into but I have a duty to love it and embrace its laws or else it's a fine or prison or worse. We have here a forced choice, one that performs a trick on the mind almost as powerful as witnessing water turn into wine. The forced choice turns what is almost an accident of nature (the fact that I was born here) into the product of my choosing and free will.

The *objet a* in the fantasy (more on this later) is designed to cover over this lack in the big Other and 'traversing the fantasy' consists in giving back to the subject this thing it introduces in the big Other to make it seem consistent. The subject learns in analysis that the thing in the big Other that fascinates him was put there by his own fantasy. In this way, analysis deprives the subject of the *jouissance* that gives his being consistency.

Trauma redux

When Žižek uses the sinking of the Titanic to illustrate Lacan's later notion of the symptom as a site of enjoyment, he evokes a fascinating theory of trauma, one that is close to Baudrillard's in his short book titled *Terrorism*. Žižek writes:

> even before it [the sinking of the *Titanic*] actually happened, there was already a place opened, reserved for it in fantasy-space. It had such a terrific impact on the 'social imaginary' by virtue of the fact that it was expected. It was foretold in amazing detail. (SOI 74)

Freud usually presents his theory of trauma – in, for instance, *Beyond the Pleasure Principle* – as something that happens as a result of the fact that one's life was unexpectedly in the balance. A soldier has a brush with death. Because he did not expect it and was not prepared for it, the event returns to haunt him in his dreams at night or it reappears in the form of symptoms. Why does it return? In order to generate the anxiety that failed to appear when his life was under threat. Anxiety would have prepared him for it. It is a defence mechanism against the unpredictable threat to life. It is a way of being prepared for the unexpected. Horror, *Schreck*, takes place whenever anxiety fails to occur and you're surprised at what happens. Žižek and Baudrillard propose a different way of looking at the matter. Baudrillard claims that a power that reigns supreme, such as the current global economic order of the West led by the United States, almost invariably evokes in everyone the unconscious fantasy of degrading and humiliating it. It solicits the infantile wish of seeing it debased or destroyed. This is why the attack on the Twin Towers on 11 September in 2001 was so shocking. It was because it was unconsciously anticipated and desired. It had been repeatedly fantasized in Hollywood action movies that stage the destruction of a major city in the United States like New York or Los Angeles. A trauma here is the result of a repressed wish finding fulfilment in actuality. It happens when what is unconsciously expected takes place. As Žižek says of the sinking of the Titanic, 'It had such a terrific impact on the "social imaginary" by virtue of the fact that it was expected.' It was anticipated in the fiction of certain authors at the turn of the nineteenth century because it was part of the *Zeitgeist*. An era was coming to an end, the age of empire from 1850 to the end of the First World War in 1918.

The other point Žižek makes relates to the photographs of the wreck at the bottom of the ocean. They exemplify a sinthome, a signifier in which the signifying function is abolished. The pictures fascinate not because of what they represent (a bygone age) but because they say nothing. We see in them a mute and 'inert presence'. The fragments of the wreck are an objectification of the libido. They are 'a kind of coagulated remnant of the liquid flux of *jouissance*, a kind of petrified forest of enjoyment'.

> The *Titanic* is a Thing in the Lacanian sense: the material leftover, the materialization of the terrifying, impossible *jouissance*. (SOI 76)

The form of ideology

Let me return to Lacan's sinthome, this signifier that functions as a site of the drive's enjoyment (*jouissance*). Žižek finds this enjoyment illustrated by the image of the wound suffered by the main character in Kafka's short story 'A Country Doctor' (SOI 82), in Wagner's *Parsifal* (SOI 83-84) and in Ridley's Scott's *Aliens*. The claim is that the subject adheres to its wound and symptom as to its very being.

> This is the symptom: an element which causes a great deal of trouble, but its absence would mean even greater trouble: total catastrophe. (SOI 85)

To unbind the trauma from the signifier – that is, the Freudian id untrammelled by the symbolic order – would result in 'pure automatism, psychic suicide, surrender to the death drive, even to the total destruction of the symbolic universe' (SOI 81). The sinthome binds the drive to a signifying formation which makes possible the primary processes, that is, combination and substitution in Lacan, condensation and displacement in Freud. The symbolic order drains the body of *jouissance* and makes life bearable, that is, less tensed and dominated by the drive.

Žižek insists on enjoyment (*jouissance*) in order to provide a final and definitive answer to the question he's been preoccupied with since his reading of Althusser in Chapter 1. Why does the subject remain wedded to what society says it is or, more precisely, to ideological state apparatuses? His answer is because of the enjoyment (*jouissance*) they procure it. We have seen that Žižek associates Kant's unconditional moral imperative – that is, the Law – with the drive and the conditional, empirical laws of the State, as well as the customs of a community, with the pleasure and reality principles. Their function is to maintain a homeostatic balance and ensure the living being's adaptation to the external world. They work towards its welfare. The drive, on the other hand, is an unconditional compulsion that makes it impossible for the pleasure and reality principles to attain the closure and satisfaction they seek, that is, the reconciliation of the psychic apparatus with the demands of social reality. The drive is the inner limit that sets the psychic apparatus eternally at odds with the exterior world (see ES 48). It is a relentless insistence on enjoyment (*jouissance*): 'social laws pacify our egotism and regulate social homeostasis; moral Law creates imbalance in this homeostasis by introducing an element of unconditional compulsion' (SOI 88). He then makes the following two observations.

(a) The *formal* character of the Law ('do your duty for duty's sake') produces enjoyment (*jouissance*). How is that to be understood? Kant contends that the categorical nature of the moral imperative resides not in its content but in its form. The moral Law has in effect no content. It is the *form of lawfulness as such*, of that which holds *without exception*. A maxim that passes the test of the categorical imperative is endowed with this very form (i.e., it holds without exception). Its constraint on the will is absolute. It is not the case that I ought not to lie because it causes harm so that if it caused no harm, it'd be morally ok to lie. Lying is intrinsically wrong. Therefore, no rational being ought to lie, no matter the circumstances and consequences. This absolute constraint forces the subject to renounce, as alternative sources of motivation, the pleasure or happiness the action may result into. At the limit, it forces the subject to renounce its welfare, at least insofar as its welfare conflicts with having to act morally – that is, if the subject has to make a choice between its life and doing what's right. Now the corollary effect of this renunciation of pleasure and happiness – that is, of doing what's right for its own sake – is enjoyment (*jouissance*). The point Žižek wants to insist on – we will see why in a moment – is that enjoyment (*jouissance*) is a by-product of renouncing one's attachment to life. It is a surplus rather than something aimed at directly.

(b) The subject remains wedded to ideology as to its very being because it procures her with this surplus-enjoyment: 'the Fascist ideology is based upon a purely formal imperative: Obey, because you must!' (SOI 89)

In Žižek's eyes, there is a structural similarity between Kant's Law and ideology. They constrain the subject to make sacrifices not for some ulterior motive but as an end in itself. You 'must find positive fulfilment in the sacrifice itself, not in its instrumental value: it is this renunciation, this giving up of enjoyment itself, which produces a certain surplus-enjoyment' (SOI 89). There is more enjoyment in making the sacrifices ideology commands of us than in receiving the rewards it promises in return for our obedience. This is the appeal of fascist ideology in distinction from the liberal ideology of instrumental reason and its concomitant scepticism about noble causes and ideals. Liberalism doesn't understand this appeal of the empty-formal character of the imperative to obey as an end itself or to sacrifice oneself for its own sake. Psychoanalysis locates in this behaviour a surplus-enjoyment. Ideology doesn't aim at some good. It aims at producing this attitude. This is why Žižek concludes the chapter by saying that 'what is really at stake in ideology is its form' (SOI 92). For it to be effective, the *jouissance* must remain hidden. The subject must believe that he is fighting for a cause. If the true aim of ideology were to be revealed to him or he was to be made aware that ideology serves only itself, then it would cease to be effective. The enjoyment (*jouissance*) would be spoilt if the subject were to become aware that the unconditional imperative serves only to bring it about. The subject must believe that he is fighting for something and that he must in consequence renounce pleasure and happiness. Only then is there surplus-enjoyment. It cannot be what is aimed at. It has to result as if by accident from realizing the cause that is aimed at.

Study questions

1. Does Žižek have good reasons for thinking that a symptom's meaning comes from the future?
2. What role does 'enjoyment' (*jouissance*) play in Žižek's understanding of ideology?

Section 3

Chapter 3 of *The Sublime Object of Ideology* is the longest. Its goal is twofold. On the one hand, Žižek's aim is to explain how sublime objects – the objects of ideology – are formed. On the other, his aim is to explore further the paradoxical character of the Real, in particular, the way it sustains the symbolic order. Laclau and Mouffe's *Hegemony and Socialist Strategy: Towards a Radical Democratic Politics*, along with the debate in analytical philosophy between the descriptivist and antidescriptivist on the question concerning the connection between words and things, is crucial for the first part of Žižek's goal. Lacan's graphs of desire – in particular, his account of the drive's enjoyment (*jouissance*) – are crucial for the second part.

In the first half of the chapter, then, Žižek focuses on the formation of the objects of ideology. In the second half, his focus is on the ideological formation of the subject. Thus, I have divided this Section under the following headings, 'The constitution of sublime objects' and 'The constitution of the subject and enjoyment (*jouissance*)'.

The constitution of sublime objects

The quilting-point: Laclau and Mouffe's hegemonic logic

For Žižek, ideology includes all three of Lacan's registers, the Symbolic, the Imaginary and the Real. One of the central features of the first is the incessant deferral of meaning ('the sliding of the signified under the signifier'). It is obvious in the common experience where one is asked for the meaning of a word and one goes looking for it in the dictionary only to be faced with the same question about a word in the *definiens*. 'What's a "bachelor"?' 'It's an unmarried man.' 'OK, but what's "unmarried" and a "man"?' and so on. A signifier refers to another which, in turn, refers to another and so on. The signified is missing – the signified that would put an end to this movement and close the symbolic on itself. The question, then, is: What renders the symbolic order – the big Other – consistent and stable? For if signifiers do not revolve around a signified, then the discourse is meaningless. It is indistinguishable from an uninterrupted sound. A signifier must be selected to play the role of signified, and it is called the 'quilting-point' or 'master signifier'. It is like the full stop at the end of the sentence that retroactively determines the meaning of its earlier parts. To put it in a catchphrase, a discourse without quilting-point(s) is without meaning.

Laclau and Mouffe's logic of hegemony follows almost naturally from this. It can be understood on the basis of the following two claims.

(a) Political struggles are like signifiers in that they are, as it were, discrete units, that is, they are logically independent of one another. There is no intrinsic connection between, say, feminism, anti-racism and ecologism. They can be combined with one another in any number of ways under liberalism, communism or fascism.

(b) Regardless of how they are combined, there is always a particular struggle that acts as the determining ground of the rest, that is, as master signifier. A political agent will subordinate her other struggles to it as to their final meaning.

Žižek writes:

> *Ecologism*, for example: its connection with other ideological elements is not determined in advance; one can be a state-oriented ecologist (if one believes that only the intervention of a strong state can save us from catastrophe), a socialist ecologist (if one locates the source of merciless exploitation of nature in the capitalist system), a conservative ecologist (if one preaches that man must again become deeply rooted in his native soil), and so on; *feminism* can be socialist, apolitical; even *racism* could be elitist or populist . . . The 'quilting' performs the totalization by means of which this free floating of ideological elements is halted, fixed – that is to say, by

> means of which they become parts of the structured network of meaning. (SOI 95-96)

A particular political struggle is like a signifier also in the sense that it is indeterminate in its identity or content so long as it is not combined with other struggles. Ideology arises with the institution of quilting-points. A quilting-point is a signifier that unifies ('quilts') discursive elements (signifiers) in a whole. Examples of quilting-points: 'the Nation', 'the People', 'our way of life', 'Democracy' and so on. These terms have in common the fact that they signify what is objectively common to everyone, a little like Rousseau's 'general will'. The 'Nation' in the modern sense denotes an everlasting political community. It exists in history, but the assumption is that it has a mythical or quasi-mythical foundation in the immemorial past and that its future is limitless.[1] Ideology and the counter-ideological tendency turn on *names*, on the kind that signify a totality and that move us to believe that it exists, and the counter-ideological suspicion that the totality – 'society', the 'Nation' and so on – doesn't exist. Ideological is the belief that society exists, that there is an actual totality of which we are part. The critique of ideology exposes the mechanisms by which the use of these names generates the belief in the existence of the thing they name. Žižek in effect holds that these terms do not refer because there is no totality out there. It is a fantasmatic object (*objet a*). Žižek's move is similar to Kant's when the latter argues, in the first *Critique*, that the world is a regulative idea, a fiction. The physical universe is part of the world, but the world itself doesn't exist. It's the setting that's necessarily presupposed by the subject's cognitive and practical enterprise.

Laclau and Mouffe propose the following as their model of political life as an alternative to classical Marxism.

> If we 'quilt' the floating signifiers through 'Communism', for example, 'class struggle' confers a precise and fixed signification to all other elements to democracy (so-called 'real democracy' as opposed to 'bourgeois formal democracy' as a legal form of exploitation); to feminism (the exploitation of women as resulting from the class-conditioned division of labour); to ecologism (the destruction of natural resources as a logical consequence to

> profit-oriented capitalist production); to the peace movement (the principal danger to peace is adventuristic capitalism), and so on. (SOI 96)

Classical Marxism claims that the economic base of society – the class conflict – plays a determining-causal role and that it is, among other things, the root of all social conflicts (gender, race, ethnicity, etc.). By resolving the class conflict, one resolves the others as well. The result is peace and social harmony. Laclau and Mouffe's objection to Marx is straightforward. They maintain against Marx (the social scientist) that there is no objective view of society – a view *sub specie aeternitatis* – that makes visible the laws it obeys. It is not because we are immersed in it that we cannot elevate ourselves above it in order to contemplate it as a whole. Society isn't an objective thing like the chair on which I am sitting or the mug out of which I drink my coffee. The courts, the police, the army (etc.) are institutions that have physical locations in a country. But they are not society. They are parts of it. But society – the whole – doesn't exist. Or rather, we should say that the existence of society is precisely what is *at stake* for political agents. They stake out its meaning or identity – what society means or should mean for everybody – each time they speak for everybody or in the name of the common good. To be precise, then, we must not say that society doesn't exist, but that its existence is symbolic. It is something *represented* by signifiers like, for instance, a country's flag, a constitution, a political discourse, the police whose function is 'to protect and serve' and so on. 'Society' (or an equivalent term that is made to stand for the whole) is the political signifier par excellence. It is the main weapon in the ideological struggle between political agents. (There is no politics where agents do not have in view the public good, where, i.e., they do not speak for everyone and, instead, it is a question of the self-interest of individuals or groups). It is the term by which are quilted discursive elements.

> In this way, every element of a given ideological field is part of a series of equivalences: its metaphorical surplus, through which it is connected with all other elements, determines retroactively its very identity (in a Communist perspective, to fight for peace *means* to fight against the capitalist order, and so on). But this enchainment is possible only on condition that a certain signifier – the Lacanian 'One' – 'quilts' the whole field and, by embodying it, effectuates its identity. (SOI 96)

'Society' is something represented by signifiers. It is represented as a unified totality. Political agents aim to make empirically real what is merely represented. They're not content to think of society as one. They want society to be one and harmonious in fact. In a democracy, that is impossible. According to Claude Lefort, democracy sustains the gap between the symbolic and empirical reality, representation and fact. In a democracy, there is a contestation for the place of power – the place from which one speaks of the public good and represents society as one – but it is a place that can be occupied temporarily. Essentially, the place of power is empty in a democracy.[2]

What does this contestation look like? A particular and contingent struggle becomes 'hegemonic' when it is passed off as the key to resolving the others, consequently, when it is passed off as universal and necessary for establishing a harmonious society. Now because society has a symbolic (representational) existence, the differences between political agents are incommensurable. It is as if each of them belonged to a different symbolic universe. The fact that they communicate with each other and seem to understand each other is an effect of language, of, that is, using similar signifiers. In truth, however, there is nothing in common between the symbolic universe of the liberal, that of the communist and that of the fascist. Their differences cannot be determined from an objective or neutral point of view. This is what Žižek, following Laclau and Mouffe, means by 'antagonism'. It is a difference for which there is no signifier – a difference, therefore, where the Real makes itself felt. In a democracy, political contestation happens across this traumatic, senseless kernel.

How are we to understand Žižek's question in the first half of Chapter 3? It turns on the relation between a certain group of names – signifiers that name the totality – and the thing they name, the public thing or *res publica*, society as an actual totality. He asks: how 'do we formulate the determining role of a particular domain without falling into a trap of essentialism?' (SOI 97). The question is actually twofold: how does essentialism spring from the use of certain terms? and how do we avoid falling prey to it? 'My thesis is that Saul Kripke's antidescriptivism offers us the conceptual tools to solve this problem' (SOI 97).

By 'essentialism' we should understand the view that (a) we rely upon a non-arbitrary distinction between the way things are and the way they appear to us, (b) things are what they are in virtue of their place and function in the whole. The matter, as I said, turns on the signifiers used to identify and name it – on, that is to say, the way we are ideologically led, in our thinking, from representing society as one to believing that it is in fact one (and that others, the pariahs and outliers in society, are impediments to its oneness and that they have, as a result, to be removed).

Descriptivism versus antidescriptivism

What links a word to a thing? Or more precisely, what links a speaker's utterance to the thing she is talking about? There are two possible views. On the one hand, we can say that her utterance is linked to the thing owing to its meaning. I will explain how in a moment. On the other, we can say that it is owing to a causal relation and baptismal act. These are the two positions in analytical philosophy and they are called, respectively, 'descriptivism' and 'antidescriptivism'.

Take the common noun 'gold'. The antidescriptivist's story is roughly the following.[3] At some far off point in the past, a speaker chose to call this yellow shiny substance by the name of 'gold' and since then people have been calling samples of it by that name. The causal chain starts from the baptismal ceremony where a mythical speaker uses the name for the very first time to denote the object (much in the way that Adam was tasked by God to name the animals). The chain extends through the generations of speakers to the speaker currently using the word in relation to a sample of the same substance. In other words, the causal relation between object and word is mediated by the communication of speakers through history. This story helps to explain, for instance, occurrences where the meaning of a word changes but the word still denotes the same thing. 'Gold' refers to gold for the antidescriptivist even if all the predicates at first attached to 'gold' are no longer attached to the current use of the word. What endures is not the description of gold but the causal link between the generations of speakers. If a scientist were to discover that gold doesn't have the properties we thought it to have when it was first discovered, we wouldn't say that the object we have been calling 'gold' is not really gold. We would say that gold doesn't possess the properties we initially thought it to have. Again, if a scientist were to find creatures that match the description of a unicorn, it doesn't follow that these creatures are unicorns. They aren't the creatures to which the word 'unicorn' was at first attached.

The descriptivist's account is different. Why do my words link up to things? Not because of an external causal relation between things and words (obvious counterexamples include mathematical and logical objects as well as imaginary ones: being non-physical, they have no causal powers and they cannot be observed) but because of the meaning associated to the words. 'Gold' refers to gold because the object fits the description. It matches the predicates connected to the word. Here the extension of the term (the number and kind of things to which it applies) is determined by its intension or meaning.

The descriptivist's theory seems to be particularly suitable for explaining why common nouns refer ('"Table" refers to tables because their properties match its description'), whereas the antidescriptivist's picture offers a sound basis for understanding why proper names attach to individuals ('We shall call him "Peter"'). However, 'both descriptivism and antidescriptivism aim at a *general* theory of referring functions'. (SOI 99) For the descriptivist, proper nouns are like common nouns. They are abbreviated or disguised descriptions. For example, 'Peter' means minimally 'the person other people refer to as "Peter"'. For the antidescriptivist, common nouns are like proper nouns. They are linked to things causally through a baptismal ceremony.

Žižek's point against the descriptivist – particularly against John Searle in *Intentionality: An Essay in the Philosophy of Mind* – is that he misses the aspect of the big Other and everything that it entails, chiefly its inherent inconsistency and contingency. It is manifest in its notion that proper names are abbreviated descriptions. The 'impersonal form ("it is called") announces the dimension of the "big Other" beyond other subjects'. (SOI 103) Moreover, this tautological description is the form taken by master signifiers, as in 'American' is 'what other people identify as "American"'. We have here a signifier without signified, a signifier, as we will see, that *creates the identity of the thing it signifies.*

The essence or *'je ne sais quoi'* of the object

Žižek's point against the antidescriptivist relates to the way the latter determines the persistence of the reference of the word in the situation where its meaning changes and the object no longer satisfies the description. The supposition is that the *identity* of the *object persists* against its changing (descriptive) properties. It is a rigid designator. The name denotes the same object in all possible worlds because it picks out its unchanging essence or quiddity, its identity.

> What is overlooked, at least in the standard version of antidescriptivism, is that this guaranteeing the identity of an object in all counterfactual situations – through a change of all its descriptive features – is *the retroactive effect of naming itself*: it is the name itself, the signifier, which supports the identity of the object. That 'surplus' in the object which stays the same in all possible worlds is 'something in it more than itself', that is to say the Lacanian *objet petit a*: we search in vain for it in positive reality because it has no positive consistency – because it is just an objectification of a void, of a discontinuity opened in reality by the emergence of the signifier. (SOI 104)

The problem for the antidescriptivist is the following. What guarantees that the name continues to refer to the thing when its meaning has changed and the thing doesn't match its descriptive features? Saul Kripke's answer is the thing's essence. There are two ways of understanding the term in philosophy.

- An essence is an attribute common to a plurality of individuals. Possessing it makes them members of the same kind. Without it, the individuals wouldn't be members of the kind. For example 'rationality' in the case of humans. To be human is to possess and exercise one's rational capacities.
- An essence picks out the property of an individual that makes it unique and different from every other member of its kind.

In the first case, we ask 'what is the essence of Socrates?' and consider what Socrates, Plato, Peter and so on, have in common. The answer will cite 'humanity' as their essence (specific difference). In the second case, we ask the same question but we mean what singles out Socrates from the rest of mankind. Here one cites 'Socrateity' as his essence (individual difference). This is what Aristotle calls *to ti ên einai* in his *Metaphysics*. It is what the individual already and always was. And it is what the rigid designator refers to. Socrateity is Socrates' transworld, rigid identity. It is, in consequence, the objective counterpart of the name's reference, its supporting ground.

It is at this point that Žižek introduces the Lacanian *objet a* as the fantasmatic object causing desire. To understand why, it is enough to recall the common view about love, that what attracts you in a person is the thing that makes her unique and incomparable, that ineffable quality or *je ne sais quoi* that distinguishes her from all the other women that are, in every other respect, exactly like her. Lacan speaks of it in Seminar eight *Transference* in his reading of Plato's *Symposium*. Alcibiades joins the company late and loudly proclaims, in his drunken state, to be head over heels for Socrates. Socrates is not particularly good-looking. But Alcibiades finds him irresistible. He detects in him something special, a treasure (*agalma*). '*Agalma*' is the object hidden in the subject that makes him desirable. It 'is the pivotal point, crux, or key of human desire'.[4] Lacan's claim is that human desire turns around a fantasmatic object. The thing causing desire is not a real quality, it is something superadded to the person by fantasy. The woman is attractive to the subject insofar as she enters the frame of his fantasy.

The objects of ideology are sublime and the cause of desire (they fascinate) because they are objects of fantasy. The ideological tendency is to say that they have a rigid identity – one that pre-exists language. The counter-ideological tendency is to say the opposite, that their identity is an effect of their name. The use of the signifier 'American' makes us believe that it denotes a rigid identity, one that is independent of the way people talk about it.

Or consider matters as follows. It is not exactly how Žižek puts it. Take a sentence in which someone says something about her identity – her racial, gender or national identity. The point is that she is not stating a fact. It is not a declarative sentence but a performative utterance like the priest's 'I now pronounce you husband and wife'. Uttered in the relevant circumstances, his words create the bond of marriage. A black man who says 'Blacks are so-and-so' isn't reporting a fact about himself. He is creating an identity. His words institute some way for him and others to be. His identity is not thinglike, it is not like a table, something you can pick apart and re-assemble at will. When we are at our ideological best, we mistake a performative utterance for a declarative sentence. We mistake a linguistic effect for an extra-linguistic fact that demarcates a group.

Identity is a linguistic construct. In naming the thing, there arises the illusion that *the thing is always identical to itself*, that it remains the same in spite of the variation of its properties. That is '*the retroactive effect of naming itself*: it is the name itself, the signifier, which supports the identity of the object' (SOI 104). The antidescriptivist fails to recognize 'the fact that naming itself retroactively constitutes its reference' (SOI 105). A thing doesn't have a rigid identity, but we are taught to think that it has one on account of the seduction of language.

Moreover, once a master signifier is instituted, individuals identify with it in order to recognize in it their own identity. The belief is that by possessing this special something, this treasure (*agalma*), they will be made whole again, they won't suffer the lack that plagues them always everywhere. Take the ad for Marlboro.

> the picture of the bronzed cowboy, the wide prairie plains, and so on – all this 'connotes', of course, a certain image of America (the land of hard, honest people, of limitless horizons . . .) but the effect of 'quilting' occurs only when a certain inversion takes place; it does not occur until 'real' Americans start to identify themselves (in their ideological self-experience) with the image created by the Marlboro advertisement – until America itself is experienced as 'Marlboro country.' (SOI 106)

The image of the Marlboro man becomes a pole of identification embodying the unchanging essence of America, 'the unattainable X, the object-cause of desire' (SOI 106).

Take another example. The typical anti-Semitic discourse represents the Jew in grotesque fashion as 'greedy', as busy with 'intrigues' and so on. It is properly anti-Semitic, however, when the proper name 'Jew' is used to denote not some descriptive quality but the ineffable something that makes Jewish people different, as when one says, 'they're greedy [etc.] *because they're Jews*.' The proper name denotes here 'that unattainable X' or 'what is "in Jew more than Jew" and which Nazism tried so desperately to seize, measure, change into a positive property enabling us to identify Jews in an objective-scientific way' (SOI 107).

Let me summarize in a few points what I have said so far about the master signifier:

- It unifies a discursive field (it is the One that unifies the Many).
- The essence it denotes is not the attribute shared by many demarcating a kind but the one that picks out the object (the individual or group) in its uniqueness and incomparableness.
- This essence is the effect of the signifier (a thing's name invariably produces the illusion that the thing is identical to itself and the same for everyone: the unity of the name seduces us into thinking that the thing is one).
- It is a fantasmatic object and the cause of the subject's desire.

Žižek writes that the 'rigid designator' – the name that picks out the thing's transworld identity – aims at 'that impossible-real kernel, at what is "in an object more than the object", at this surplus produced by the signifying operation' (SOI 107). What is 'in me more than myself'? Nothing at all. The fantasmatic object is the *objectification of the subject's lack*. Let us recall that what the subject desires in the Other is *itself*. The *objet a* is the piece of the Real it no longer enjoys because it's been alienated from it but that (it thinks that) it can re-find in the Other.

Moreover, if it's a question of naming the traumatic Real, it is clear that there are countless ways of doing so. The key to Marechal Pétain's success in 1940, for instance, is that his interpretation of the trauma of the defeat prevailed. What

> had been experienced a moment ago as traumatic, incomplete loss became readable, obtained meaning. But the point is that this symbolization was not inscribed in the Real itself: never do we reach the point at which 'the circumstances themselves begin to speak', the point at which language starts to function immediately as 'language of the Real': the predominance of Pétain's symbolization was a result of a struggle for ideological hegemony. (SOI 107)

What unifies and makes intelligible a historical situation is a signifier rather than some event, meaning or idea. Žižek's suggestion is that any signifier would do. There is no necessary connection between the name and the situation it names. It is arbitrary.

We can now return to the question raised earlier. How do Laclau and Mouffe's logic of hegemony avoid the trap of essentialism? For the essentialist, terms like 'democracy', 'socialism' or 'fascism' refer to inherent properties that institutions ought to have in order to qualify as 'democratic', 'socialist' or 'fascist'. It's a question of how to define these terms and how to classify things under them. Laclau and Mouffe deny the view that these terms pick out inherent properties.

> In the last resort, the only way to define 'democracy' is to say that it contains all political movements and organizations which legitimize, designate themselves as 'democratic'; the only way to define 'Marxism' is to say that this term designates all movements and theories which legitimize themselves through reference to Marx, and so on. In other words, the only possible definition of an object in its identity is that this is the object which is always designated by the same signifier – tied to the same signifier. It is the signifier which constitutes the kernel of the object's 'identity'. (SOI 108-109)

How is the critic of ideology to read words like 'democracy'? As would a nominalist. 'Democracy', 'socialism' and the like mean nothing in themselves. A movement or group calls itself with one of these names, and in thus calling itself, the illusion arises that it picks out an unchanging essence. There is, for instance, nothing in common between the democracy practiced in liberal Western societies and the democracy of the former Soviet Union, 'socialist democracy'. And because there is nothing in common between them, we lack the ground for saying that the one is the perverted, degenerate form of the other and so on. If 'democracy' is not defined by a positive content; if, instead, it is defined by its opposition, in the network of signifiers, to what is 'not democratic'; and if, finally and as a result, the signification of 'democracy' shifts each time something else is brought under what is 'not democratic', then there is no invariable – that is to say, objective – standard by which to judge whether one is true and the other false. Where does that leave us? With a performative understanding of assertions of identity. What is democratic (or socialist, or feminist, etc.) is constituted by its utterance or chosen signifier and outside of it it has no meaning: 'its signification coincides with its own act of enunciation'. The role of master signifier is 'purely structural, its nature is purely performative'.

> A 'Jew', for example, is in the last resort one who is stigmatized with the signifier 'Jew'; all the phantasmic richness of the traits supposed to characterize Jews (avidity, the spirit of intrigue, and so on) is here to conceal not the fact that 'Jews are really not like that', not the empirical reality of Jews, but the fact that in the anti-Semitic construction of a 'Jew', we are concerned with a purely structural function. (SOI 109-110)

We fail to note the performative character of the anti-Semite's discourse.

One final remark about the master signifier in relation to the suggestive example Žižek cites in *The Parallax View*. It illustrates how a signifier unifies and brings order to a situation rife with conflicts, confusion and uncertainties. We are asked to imagine a situation of social disintegration where the cohesive power of ideology is in retreat. In such a situation, the master is he who invents a signifier and stabilizes the situation by means of it. He makes order out of chaos. He renders the situation transparent and readable.

> Think about anti-Semitism in 1920s Germany: people experienced themselves as disoriented, thrown into undeserved military defeat, an economic crisis which eroded away their life savings, political inefficiency, moral degeneration . . . and the Nazis provided a single agent which accounted for it all – the Jew, the Jewish plot. Therein lies the magic of a Master: although there is nothing new at the level of positive content, nothing is quite the same after he pronounces his word. (PV 37)

If the situation comprises a multitude of issues causing fear, the master signifier makes it possible to exchange the many fears for one fear, in this case, for the fear of the Jew as cause of the economic crisis, the defeat, the moral degeneration of society and so on.

The constitution of the subject and enjoyment (*jouissance*)

Imaginary and symbolic identification

Does the master signifier abolish 'the endless floating of signifiers without residue? If not, how do we conceive the dimension which escapes it?' (SOI 111)

The general claim of the second half of Chapter 3 is that what escapes the signifier at the same time supports it. This is, as we know, the function exercised by the Real of the drive, *jouissance*, fantasy – in short, by what we find indicated on the upper level of Lacan's third and fourth graphs of desire. Regarding Žižek's reading of the first graph (SOI 111-112), it is important to keep in mind that the subject's entrance into society via the big Other (the battery of signifiers) coincides with ideological interpellation and misrecognition (see Figure 3.3.1).

Regarding his reading of the second graph (SOI 114), let me make the following observations. The master signifier holds the place of the big Other (the O in the graph). The big Other is society. It is embodied in authority figures that represent it. s(O) on the left is the meaning (signified) retroactively constituted by the master signifier (O). The vector s(O)-O terminates in 'Voice' which Žižek interprets as the object that remains after the master signifier has fixed the meaning of neighbouring signifiers. What remains is a 'hypnotic voice'.

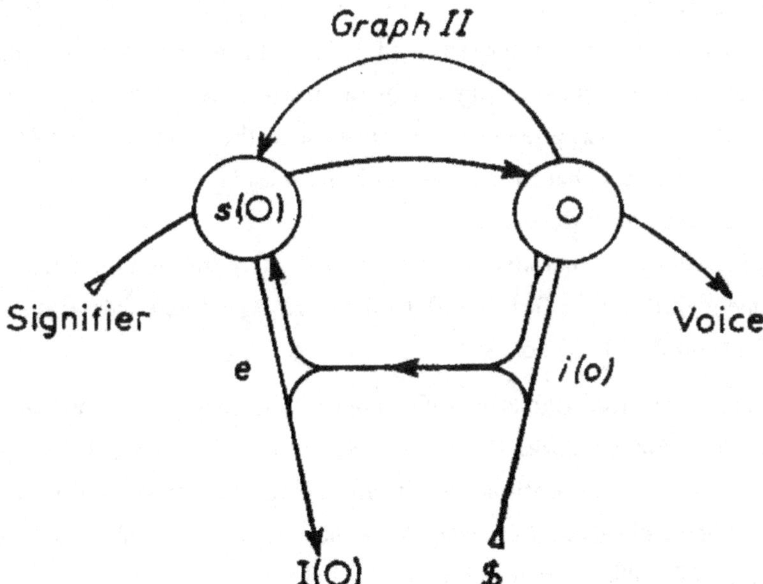

Figure 3.3.1 *Graph of desire, Jacques Lacan, Ecrits, trans. Bruce Fink (New York: W.W. Norton & Company, 2006), p. 435.*

> when the same word is repeated to us indefinitely we become disoriented, the word loses the last traces of its meaning, all that is left is its inert presence exerting a kind of somniferous hypnotic power. (SOI 115)

Or think of the superego or the so-called 'voice of conscience'. Because the voice by which it addresses the subject is not attached to the body of a particular person, its origin is unlocalizable. It comes neither from within the subject nor from outside of it in someone else. That is why it does not cease to disturb the subject in its self-presence. The voice is an object and piece of the Real, a remainder of the process of symbolization. (See 'The Undergrowth of Enjoyment: How Popular Culture can Serve as an Introduction to Lacan' in ZR.)

The second graph begins with the barred subject at the bottom right. It traverses the chain of signifiers (O) and terminates at point I(O) at the bottom left. The symbol 'I(O)' stands for symbolic identification or Ego Ideal. The subject identifies with a trait (I) that makes the other person the representative of an institution or the symbolic order. The trait 'assumes concrete, recognizable shape in a name or in a mandate that the subject takes upon himself and/or that is bestowed on him'. (SOI 116) This is to be distinguished from imaginary identification that takes place along the vector e-i(o) linking the imaginary ego and its imaginary counterpart or Ideal Ego. This is Lacan's mirror phase. The infant sees an image of himself in the mirror. He seems to himself to be autarchic and independent. He identifies with the image in spite of – or because of – the fact that he experiences himself as dependent on his mother and as helpless before the drive.

The ideological formation of the subject takes place through imaginary and symbolic identification. To this end, let me clarify the difference between the Ego Ideal and the Ideal Ego.

> imaginary identification is identification with the image in which we appear likeable to ourselves, with the image representing 'what we would like to be', and symbolic identification, identification with the very place *from where* we are being observed, *from where* we look at ourselves so that we appear to ourselves likeable, worthy of love. (SOI 116)

The imaginary comprises relations of likeness and unlikeness. It includes the field of poetry from which some animals are also not exempt. The Symbolic comprises differential relations, oppositional terms, signifiers. The Real is the limit of the Symbolic. It is where the drive obtains enjoyment (*jouissance*). The Ideal Ego is the imaginary pole of identification. It is literally what its expression suggests, the *ideal* ego, what I would like to be and what, in being it, makes me likeable in my own eyes. What ideal does it portray? The classical enlightenment one: be independent, be the author of your thoughts and actions, be an agent. Imaginary identification is identification with this image, and it is tantamount to a misrecognition, for the subject takes herself to be what she is not.

Symbolic identification is identification with a signifier (rather than with an image). The signifier in question is the Name-of-the-Father. By identifying with it, the subject secures a symbolic position(s) in society. He becomes the representative of an institution, community, race, family and so on. The full force of Lacan's definition of the signifier comes into play here as 'that which represents a subject for another signifier'. The subject always also speaks for others even when she speaks for herself. Besides, the big Other is for the subject its central point of reference: by identifying with the signifier, I identify with the place from where the Other observes what I say and do. So, for example, if I give alms to the poor, that is partly because it elevates me in the big Other's esteem. It is a question of becoming worthy of the big Other's love. Parental figures are a stand-in for objectivity and truth. If I observe myself from the standpoint of the big Other, that is because I want to ascertain my objective worth, that is, my worth in everyone's eyes. Kant brings this point home in the opening passages of the *Groundwork for the Metaphysics of Morals* when he writes that I cannot judge whether I am worthy of being happy except from the point of view of 'an impartial rational spectator', that is, God.

The subject has an imaginary and symbolic existence, then, and the question we should ask ourselves when the subject identifies with an image – say, with a football player or popstar – is: from what point of view does its imaginary identification appear likeable? *For whom* is it identifying with a footballer or popstar? That is to say that imaginary identification is subordinate to symbolic identification. It is in order to appear likeable to the big Other that the subject identifies with a certain image rather than with another. The difference between imaginary and symbolic identification is the difference, in the second graph, between i(o) and I(O). i(o) is subordinated to I(O): 'it is the symbolic identification (the point from which we are observed) which dominates and determines the image, the imaginary form in which we appear to ourselves likeable' (SOI 120). This interplay of imaginary and symbolic identification integrates the subject in a socio-symbolic network.

'*Che vuoi?*'

Identification doesn't take place without producing a remainder that refuses to be integrated in the socio-symbolic network. That remainder is what Lacan situates on the upper part of the graph centred on the question '*Che vuoi?*', 'What do you want?' (see Figure 3.3.2).

Recall that O is the big Other. The desire of the Other is marked by the small *d* on the right hand side. It is located where the question escapes the symbolic order. 'What does the Other want (from me)?' is the ineluctable question plaguing the subject from infancy onwards. The subject forms her fantasy – which, in turn, gives shape to her desire – in response to it. The formula of fantasy appears on the left hand side as ($ <> o).

Why does this question plague the subject? Let me take a detour by way of Freud and Laplanche on the theory of seduction. In the 'Third Essay' of his *Three Essays on the Theory of Sexuality* (1905), Freud considers almost in passing the unconscious effect of the mother's action on her infant when she bathes him. He is bound to be struck by the question 'What does she want from me (apart from simply to wash me)?' on account of the pleasurable excitations she produces on the surface of his body. A mother regards her child 'with feelings that are derived from her own sexual life: she strokes him, kisses him, rocks him and quite clearly treats him as a substitute for a complete sexual object'.

> A mother would probably be horrified if she were made aware that all her marks of affection were rousing her child's sexual instinct and preparing for its later intensity. She regards what she does as asexual, 'pure' love, since, after all, she carefully avoids applying more excitations to the child's genitals than are unavoidable in nursery care.[5]

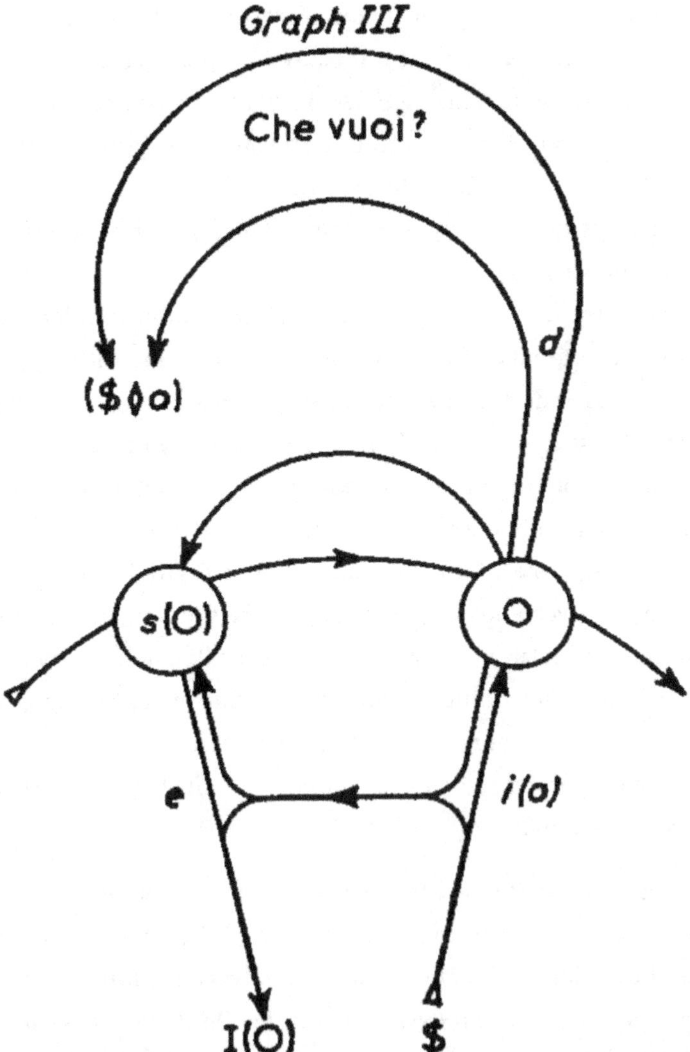

Figure 3.3.2 *Graph of desire, Jacques Lacan, Ecrits, trans. Bruce Fink (New York: W.W. Norton & Company, 2006), p. 435.*

The sexual-seductive significance of the mother's caresses and kisses lies in the fact that they are *not* transparent, neither to the little boy nor to the mother. 'The "attentions of a mother" or the "aggression of a father" are seductive only because they are not transparent. They are seductive because they are opaque, because they convey something enigmatic.'[6] The mother has no intention of seducing her infant. Nevertheless, it invariably happens as a result of the fact that her actions cause him pleasure. Her hands quite literally inscribe an enigmatic signifier on his body, 'What does she want from me?', the infant cannot symbolize let alone answer. It insists as a signifier without signified. It is pushed back in the unconscious. According to Laplanche, it is the primally repressed signifier, the thing constitutive of the repressed unconscious.

Let us look at it from the point of view of the symbolic order. We know that its positions are inherently contingent. The academic title of professor, for instance, is the effect of a set of rituals and performatives belonging to the modern, that is to say, the early-nineteenth-century university. The same is true of the title of king or ambassador or of one's relationship status, that is, 'married', 'single', 'divorced' and so on. None of these positions have a substantive content, one whose meaning could be derived from the position itself or from the psychobiological organism of the speaker. They are the effect of contingent social relations. That is why there is ultimately no answer to the question 'Why am I this thing – a professor – which you, the big Other, say that I am?' The subject cannot justify her place in the world because there is nothing grounding it. Or rather, what grounds it – the big Other – is in itself groundless and lacking.

> The subject does not know why he is occupying this place in the symbolic network. His own answer to this '*Che vuoi?*' of the Other can only be the hysterical question: 'Why am I [a teacher, a master, a king . . . or George Kaplan]?' Briefly: '*Why am I what you [the big Other] are saying that I am?*' And the final moment of the psychoanalytic process is, for the analysand, precisely when he gets rid of this question – that is, when he accepts his being as *non-justified by the big Other*.

We saw at the end of Section 1 why Žižek identifies the critical attitude with hysteria rather than with perversion. He wonders here whether hysteria is the effect of a failed interpellation; 'what is the hysterical question if not an articulation of the incapacity of the subject to fulfil the symbolic identification, to assume fully and without restraint the symbolic mandate?' (SOI 126).

Fantasy

Fantasy is the subject's response to the unknowable '*Che vuoi?*' and its way of masking the inconsistency of the big Other. The subject doesn't know what he should be because he doesn't know what the Other desires (from him). Fantasy steps in to escape this deadlock. It tells the subject what would fill the Other's lack (the *objet a*) in such a way that the subject can position himself in relation to it. Either it is the thing the subject wants to be in order to complete the Other, or it is the thing he wants to recover from the Other, believing that the Other has stolen it from him. Such is the logic of the racist's discourse. For the anti-Semite, it is never clear what the Jew wants – 'his actions are always suspected of being guided by some hidden motives (the Jewish conspiracy, world domination and the moral corruption of Gentiles, and so on)'. Fantasy fills the void opened by the Other's desire

> by giving us a definite answer to the question 'What does the Other want?', it enables us to evade the unbearable deadlock in which the Other wants something from us, but we are at the same time incapable of translating this desire of the Other into a positive interpellation, into a mandate with which to identify. (SOI 128)

Žižek suspects that Jews are the pre-eminent objects of racism because of their God which embodies this terrifying void that is the Other's desire 'with the formal prohibition on "making an image of God" – on filling out the gap of the Other's desire with a positive fantasy-scenario'. It is a God whose desire remains unknowable.

> The basic position of a Jewish believer is, then, that of Job: not so much lamentation as incomprehension, perplexity, even horror at what the Other (God) wants with the series of calamities that are being inflicted upon him. (SOI 128-129)

Christianity, the religion of love, is, by contrast, bent on hiding the lack. The penitent is intent on sacrificing himself to and for the Other. He presents himself as the object that will fill the Other's lack – as the object, that is, of the Other's desire. That is what love amounts to for Lacan. It is the (narcissistic) idea that the one completes the other, that the one is a part of the other. The penitent behaves like the lover to his beloved. He thinks to himself 'You complete me; I fulfil myself in giving myself to you' and so on. 'Christianity is therefore to be conceived as an attempt to "gentrify" the Jewish "*Che vuoi?*" through the act of love and sacrifice' (SOI 130). Sacrifice creates the impression of annulling both lacks, the desire of the subject and the desire of the Other.

Fantasy is usually thought of as a substitute satisfaction for a desire that cannot be met in reality. For example, the infant wants to suckle the breast. The breast is not available. The infant is given a dummy instead or it sucks its thumb. For Lacan, fantasy frames desire: '*through fantasy, we learn "how to desire"*' (SOI 132). Its function is twofold:

- It conceals the unbearable lack in the big Other by telling the subject what it wants.
- It tells the subject what to desire and how.

This is why the concluding moment of therapy involves renouncing the scenarios of fantasy and allowing oneself to become exposed to the lack of the big Other. Lacan's formula in Seminar seven *The Ethics of Psychoanalysis* 'not to give way on one's desire' means: renounce the fantasies by which you occlude the Other's desire. The subject is brought to the point where he must renounce being the *objet a* for the Other.

Freud's claim in his *Three Essays on the Theory of Sexuality* that desire does not have an object to which it is naturally attached – its object is arbitrary – raises the obvious question: well, then, what attaches desire to this person rather than to that one? Why do I love this woman rather than that one? Žižek-Lacan's answer is that the first woman has entered the subject's frame of fantasy. Unless that happens, the subject cannot find her attractive. She must embody that *je ne sais quoi* that drives the subject up the wall – that alienated part of the subject whose repossession he thinks will make him whole again. In the third version of the graph, this *je ne sais quoi* is the *o* in the formula of fantasy. It is the *objet a*.

> how does an empirical, positively given object become an object of desire; how does it begin to contain some X, some unknown quality, something

> which is 'in it more than it' and makes it worthy of our desire? By entering the framework of fantasy, by being included in a fantasy-scene which gives consistency to the subject's desire. (SOI 133)

This is linked to the psychoanalytic doxa that a man looks for a woman who unconsciously reminds him of his mother. Why his mother? Because she represents the agency responsible for the subject's first experience of pleasure and satisfaction during infancy that initiated his sexual life. His sexual life consists in re-finding this original satisfaction with substitutes. Lacan adds to it the idea that the mother is reduced, in the subject's fantasy, to a cluster of signifiers and that if the woman embodying them is in effect too close to them herself, she provokes revulsion. The signifiers exert a power of attraction from a distance only. That is to say, the subject responds in one of two ways to the object of its desire.

(a) The woman who enters the frame of my fantasy fascinates me. She becomes the object of my desire by embodying symbolic traits that make her a substitute of my mother, that is, of this object that furnished the subject primal satisfaction and that the subject aims to recover through this substitute.

(b) If the woman is too close to the maternal Thing, if she is immediately attached to it, then desire is suffocated by 'incestuous claustrophobia' and she inspires disgust.

Either she attracts me because she embodies a symbolic trait of the maternal Thing, or she repulses me because she is too closely attached to it. The Other is a source of attraction and repulsion insofar as she embodies the maternal Thing or its leftover, the *objet a*.

The Real

Let us move on to the fourth graph. What completes it is the vector of enjoyment (*jouissance*) on the upper part crossing through the symbolically constituted desire of the Other (see Figure 3.3.3).

The upper level is that of bodily *jouissance*, the lower level that of the symbolic and imaginary constitution of the subject. The effect of the signifier

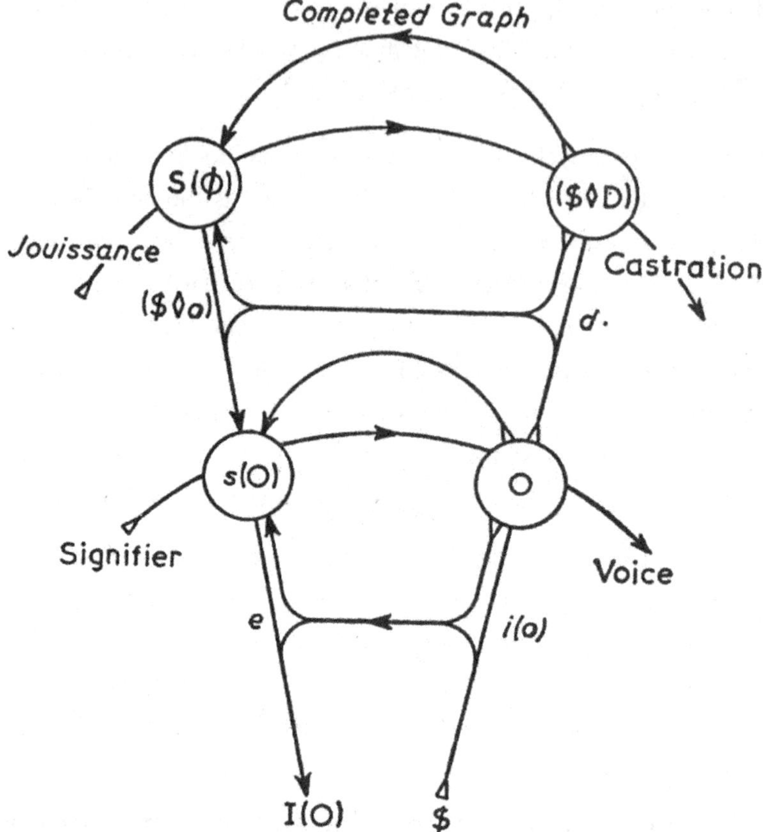

Figure 3.3.3 *Graph of desire, Jacques Lacan, Ecrits, trans. Bruce Fink (New York: W.W. Norton & Company, 2006), p. 435.*

on the body is to drain it of enjoyment (*jouissance*), 'the body is submitted to *castration*, enjoyment is evacuated from it'.

> In other words, the order of the signifier (the big Other) and that of enjoyment (the Thing as its embodiment) are radically heterogeneous, inconsistent; any accordance between them is structurally impossible. (SOI 136-137)

($ <> D) on the right hand side is the formula of the drive. The point is that as Žižek explains (SOI 138), the evacuation of enjoyment is never complete. There are remainders. These are the erogenous zones, the areas susceptible of powerful excitations. The D (symbolic demand) denotes the erogenous zones. It is useful to recall here the scene of seduction where the mother, by washing her infant, creates those zones. The erogenous zones are not limited to the usual three: oral, anal, genital. It can include the neck or nose; any area of the body is eroticized as a result of bearing the enigmatic signifier 'What does she want from me?' The point is that the erogenous zones aren't differentiated by nature so much as by the signifier.

S(Ø) on the upper left hand side is the signifier of the lack in the Other. It is a function of the fact that the Other is penetrated by senseless enjoyment. The signifier of the Other's enjoyment represents its inconsistency: the big Other is barred or non-full, it is the opposite of a self-contained, autonomous totality. If the symbolic order were a closed structure, then the only option for the subject would be for it to be the phallus of the big Other, the thing that completes it. If the big Other is lacking, that is because it doesn't have the thing that would complete it. It is like the subject blocked and desiring. Žižek introduces Lacan's notion of separation here, which can mean two things:

- The big Other is separated from the phallus that would complete it and render it consistent and full.
- The subject constitutes her desire independently of the Other's desire. This is the position occupied by the subject that has come out of the Oedipal complex and that no longer desires to be the object of the (m) Other's desire (her imaginary phallus).

Separation involves the subject's recognition that the Other doesn't have the phallus and that it is also lacking and desiring (it). 'This lack in the Other gives the subject – so to speak – breathing space.' It allows him to identify 'with the lack in the Other' (SOI 137). Generally speaking, however, the subject experiences his symbolically structured environment (the big Other) as consistent, meaningful and full by concealing, with the help of fantasies, the fact that it is lacking and inconsistent and that it is inconsistent on account of the fact that it is penetrated by senseless enjoyment.

Ideology revisited

We already know the significance of the upper level of the graph for Žižek. It is the level that usually escapes the critique of ideology on account of the fact that it exceeds interpellation and the symbolic and imaginary constitution of the subject. The weakness Žižek detects in Althusser as well as in Laclau and Mouffe is their limitation to the lower level of the graph. Totalitarianism shows clearly that ideology involves more than the totalization of a discursive field by means of quilting-points. The 'last support' of the subject's attachment to the signifier is 'the nonsensical, pre-ideological kernel of enjoyment' (SOI 140). The critique of ideology has to operate in two registers:

- Its function is, in the first place, to expose the master signifiers that organize the surface of the ideological text and show how they work.
- Its function is also to expose the kernel of enjoyment ideology produces by means of fantasy.

The following serves as an example of how the analysis of anti-Semitism can proceed. The critical standard is Laclau's contention that society doesn't exist. It casts the right kind of light on anti-Semitism. Žižek infers from it that 'the Jew is its symptom'. It is the figure through which the nonexistence of society is repressed. The analysis proceeds in two steps following the two levels of the graph of desire. At the discursive level, it's a matter of identifying how the primary processes – displacement and condensation – are at work in repressing the fact that society doesn't exist.

1. Social antagonism – that is, the fact that society is inherently lacking and inconsistent – is displaced onto the antagonism between the homogenous texture of the social body and the Jew as its corrupting cause and influence. This allows us to deny that society is *a priori* impossible and to say instead that the Jew is an empirical obstacle to the realization of society as an organic totality.

The 'figure of the Jew condenses opposing features, features associated with lower and upper classes'. For example, they are dirty *and* intellectual, voluptuous *and* impotent and so on. Such a constructed figure is a symptom 'in the sense of a coded message, a cypher, a disfigured representation of social antagonism' (SOI 141).

2. This analysis of the ideological text isn't enough because it doesn't explain why the figure of the Jew captures our desire. To this end,

> we must see it as having entered the frame of fantasy structuring the drive's enjoyment (*jouissance*). That is to say, we must look on the figure of the Jew as embodying, in a repressed or disavowed fashion, the nonexistence of the big Other, the senseless traumatic kernel that makes harmony, unity, fullness and so on, *a priori* impossible. The figure of the Jew is the site where enjoyment (*jouissance*) erupts – in the strict clinical sense, it is a symptom.

Žižek adds in respect of this second moment that fantasy 'is precisely the way the antagonistic fissure is masked. In other words, *fantasy is a means for an ideology to take its own failure into account*'. (SOI 142). 'Society is not prevented from achieving its full identity because of Jews: it is prevented by its own antagonistic nature, by its own immanent blockage, and it "projects" this internal negativity into the figure of the "Jew"' (SOI 143).

The logic of ideological fantasy can be described roughly as follows:

- An inner deadlock (the drive) prevents society from coinciding with itself and existing as a totality. This deadlock is displaced onto the outsider who is taken to be responsible for society's failure to achieve harmony. From this it follows that the harmony can be restored by eliminating the outsider. A structural or inner impossibility becomes a contingent, external accident whose removal can restore peace and order.

If the figure of the Jew is a symptom, that is because it is a product of society. It is not an aberrant deviation. Reading the symptom is key to understanding how it works and fails.

Study questions

1. What is the ideological significance of quilting-points for Žižek?
2. What is the ideological significance of fantasy and the drive for Žižek?

Section 4

Žižek lays out his theory of ideology in the first three chapters of *The Sublime Object of Ideology*. In Chapter 4 he considers its limits and the extent to which the Real intervenes in and upends the symbolic. To this end, he offers a reading of Walter Benjamin's *Theses on the History of Philosophy* in order to showcase the revolutionary promise borne by historical materialism and the now (*Jetztzeit*). He concludes the Chapter by introducing an aspect of Claude Lefort's notion of formal democracy – the practice of voting – as another instance of the Real's intrusion in the symbolic. This is done in the background of his distinction, at the start of the Chapter, between symbolic and physical death. This is what I propose to start with.

Symbolic and physical existence: Symbolic and physical death

Žižek begins Chapter 4 by distinguishing between three stages in Lacan's thinking of the relation between the death drive and the signifier.

(a) The first period – the reference point is Lacan's 1953 Rome Discourse, *The Function and the Field of Speech and Language in Psychoanalysis* – is marked by Hegel's thesis from the section titled 'Sense-Certainty' in the *Phenomenology of Spirit*, according to which the word is the death of the thing. What does that mean? Hegel shows in the section that the philosophical and epistemic position of the empirical realist is inconsistent – the position that maintains that the things we perceive exist independently of the mind just as we perceive them and that we know them immediately, simply by opening our eyes, as it were, and saying what we see. According to this position, sensible individuals alone exist, this table, this horse and so on. To show that this position is inconsistent, Hegel asks the empirical realist to describe her knowledge of sensible individuals. How does she know this table, this horse? Hegel's point is not only that what I know of an individual are its properties, which have the logical structure of universals – 'this horse is brown', 'this horse has a mane' where 'brown' and 'mane' are universals, that is, terms that apply in the same sense to a plurality of individuals. Even to fix the individual as the object of my discourse – as the thing I am talking about – I have to use indexicals, which are relative, formal-empty and universal. Someone says to the empirical realist: 'You say *this* horse. But what do you mean by "this"?' She says: 'Well by *this* I mean the horse *here* and *now*.' But here and now have a quasi-unlimited extension: they don't simply pick out your horse, they pick out any individual in space and time. So while you mean this one, the terms at your disposal don't help you say what you mean. In effect, they mean the opposite of what you mean to say. Language betrays your meaning or intention. What it says (the universal) is the truth and it is in contradiction with your position. The moment you begin to talk, the individual you talk about has as it were volatilized in the web of universal terms that governs your discourse and all you really get hold of is a universal or generic 'This,' 'Here' and 'Now.'

This is roughly how the empirical realist is led to concede that universals are not only necessary conditions of knowledge, but that they are also built into the logical structure of individuals. After all, if an individual is known through its properties, is that not because an individual is a sum of properties, that is, because it is a *one equal to many*? Or is it a one that is a substratum, something that underlies the properties and that is in addition to them? and so on. That brings the *Phenomenology of Spirit* to the next shape of consciousness, that of perception, which explores the possible combinations between the one and the many in the context of empirical realism and its theory of knowledge.

The lesson Lacan draws from Hegel's demonstration is that (1) what persists is not the individual, this table; this table, being a physical thing, perishes away (nothing remains the same in space and time); what persists is the universal 'table'; (2) in what sense does it persist? Not in any physical sense, of course. 'Table' is the truth of individual tables: what endures is their notion or intelligibility or, speaking Platonically, their essence. Put differently, the meaning of 'table' represents what a table is, its social function, in the absence of actual tables. The 'appearance of the table itself is already marked with a certain lack – to know what a table is, what it means, we must have recourse to the word which implies an absence of the thing' (SOI 145). In what sense does the word imply the absence of the thing? Žižek does not say. It is suggested by the standard definition of the sign as what represents the thing in its absence. Derrida's argument in 'Signature Event Context' is of help here. The question is: what makes a linguistic sign – any mark whatever – universally communicable, that is, communicable as the same for everyone? The answer is its re-identifiability as the same across possible contexts. If the unity or identity of the name were dependent upon the thing it names, then it wouldn't be communicable, for the absence of the thing would entail the absence of the name. Hence, if the name is to be universally communicable, it must be possible to re-identify it as the same in the absence of what it names. The implication is that a signifier has an ideal existence or it has none at all.

(b) In Lacan's second period – marked by his reading of Poe's 'Purloined Letter' in 1956 – death is linked not to speech but to the structure of language. What kind of structure does language have? It is a 'senseless autonomous mechanism'. Language is a system of differential elements (signifiers) that are combined with and substituted for one another. It creates syntagmatic and paradigmatic connections. Signifiers are associated laterally and vertically. This associative process is random and automatic and generates patterns. Chance is the agency of the signifier and its results, naturally, are unexpected, sometimes erratic and funny, at other times a danger to the living being inasmuch as it upends its homeostatic balance and adaptation to its external environment. The operative opposition here is between the *death drive qua the structure of language* and *the register of the imaginary* governed by the pleasure and reality principles. As already mentioned, both principles are not opposed in Lacan. One is in the service of the other. The pleasure principle reduces tension to a minimum in the psychic apparatus or it keeps it constant. The reality principle aims at the living being's adaptation, it aims at its living in agreement with the demands of reality. At this stage of Lacan's itinerary, both principles are discharged by the imaginary whereas the symbolic order, which coincides with the death drive, builds up tension and deregulates the living being.

(c) In Lacan's third and final period, which begins with his 1959–60 Seminar 7 *The Ethics of Psychoanalysis*, the principal opposition is not between the imaginary and the symbolic but between the symbolic and the Real. The symbolic order now coincides with the pleasure principle and the Real of bodily enjoyment with the death drive. In Seminar 7, Lacan calls the Real 'the Thing'. The Thing is both the drive and the maternal body from which the subject is cut off (castration) as a result of the signifier. It is for the subject a pole of attraction and repulsion. Union with it – incestual union – is tantamount to psychotic autism, the destruction of the split subject qua subject of the unconscious. The psychotic subject has no unconscious.

> The symbolic order is striving for a homeostatic balance, but there is in its kernel, at its very centre, some strange, traumatic element which cannot be symbolized, integrated into the symbolic order – the Thing. (SOI 147)

Lacan describes the Thing as an 'extimacy' in order to highlight the fact that it is in the subject like an internal foreign body potentially having pathogenic effects. What is most intimate to the subject – the Thing or death drive – is symbolically inassimilable. The drive's unfettered enjoyment invites symbolic death, 'the radical annihilation of the symbolic texture through which so-called reality is constituted'.

> The very existence of the symbolic order implies a possibility of its radical effacement, of 'symbolic death' – not the death of the so-called 'real object' in its symbol, but the obliteration of the signifying network itself. (SOI 147)

The point is that the destruction of the symbolic order *cannot be symbolized.* It is possible to speak about the destruction of humans, animals and plants. It is possible to think away life on earth. It is even possible to envisage the destruction of the entire physical universe in some major cataclysmic event, in the antithesis of the Big Bang, say, the Big Boom. But what is not possible, what is impossible *de jure*, is to signify the abolition of the signifier. As long as there is a signifier to represent it, it is not with the *remainderless destruction of the signifying network* that we are concerned with. Žižek's argument is Heidegger-inspired. Death, the possibility of the absolute impossibility of Dasein, cannot be represented. It gives Dasein nothing to think about. It is nothing but an anticipatory horizon; it gives the subject nothing to actualize. In other words, the abolition of all archives, of the symbolic order as such, lacks a signified. That is why the symbolic order is inherently open and inconsistent. Conversely, this very lack of a signified is the impetus to symbolize what there is.

These three stages imply three different ways of thinking about the concluding moment of the psychoanalytic cure:

(a) Symptoms in Lacan's first stage are imaginary elements that have not been symbolized. To symbolize them, to integrate them into one's history and world, is to liberate oneself from their pathogenic effect. Analysis 'gives meaning, retroactively, to what was in the beginning a meaningless trace' (SOI 147). The final moment thus involves being able to tell one's story to the Other seamlessly.

(b) Where the symbolic order coincides with the death drive, the symbolic order imposes on the subject a loss – symbolic castration – and the final moment of analysis consists in accepting it. (What does symbolic castration deprive me of? The position of being the mother's imaginary phallus. What does that mean? At the pre-Oedipal stage, the subject desires to be what the mother desires (I relate to her desire). This is the imaginary phallus. It is the object of the mother's desire and the child wants to be it. The father or the person exercising the paternal function intervenes as a third between mother and child. He prohibits the mother from making her child her imaginary phallus, the thing that will make her whole. The child eventually recognizes that his mother doesn't have 'it' (after all, that is what she desires, and if she desires it, that is because she doesn't have 'it'), that he (the child) also doesn't have 'it', and that the father has 'it'. In short, the child gives up his desire of being the mother's imaginary phallus. To make up for his lack, he identifies with the father: 'I will be like him because he has "it" and having "it" will make me loveable in the eyes of the big Other.' And so begins the search for the symbolic phallus for the male, that is, of the signifier whose possession gives the subject the impression of having 'it' – 'it' being authority, power, fullness and so on – when, of course, the signifier is a pretence of authority, power and fullness.

Thus, we can say that the imaginary phallus = an *imagined object*. It is of the same kind as the specular image the infant has of himself as being one and whole. It grounds and governs his relations to reality. Whereas the symbolic phallus = a *signifier* signifying signification in general. Having it or wanting to have it defines the masculine position. Being it defines the feminine position.)

At this second stage of Lacan's thought, analysis terminates when the subject consents to being symbolically castrated 'as a price to be paid for access to his desire'. It is insofar as the subject gives up being the mother's imaginary phallus that he carves out a space for *his* desire. Symbolic castration is the price he pays for his relative independence. It is the necessary condition for entering the symbolic order.

(c) In the third and final stage of Lacan's thought, the symbolic order is conceived as lacking, as riven by the Real. The symbolic order has its limit in the drive. The subject comes to terms with it by means of fantasy, which distorts the lack in the Other and protects the subject from its traumatic effects. This is why analysis terminates by 'going through the fantasy'. The subject recognizes that there is nothing behind the fantasy save the 'nothing' of the Other's desire. It is a question of acknowledging the unbearable lack in the Other. The subject understands that 'the fantasy is a construction whose function is to hide this void, this "nothing" – that is, the lack in the Other' (SOI 148). More on this in a moment.

It is possible to see from here on what Žižek-Lacan mean by the idea of two deaths. 'In a way, everybody must die twice.' Consider for the purposes of illustration the king's body. Effectively, according to Ernst Kantorowicz's *The King's Two Bodies*, the king has two bodies. He has a natural body according to which he gets hungry, cold, has particular needs and ailments and so on. The death of the natural body is just that, the king's natural death. But the king also has a symbolic body that consists of the laws and tradition that unify the kingdom, its history from its mythical birth and its interminable longevity: the king never dies. More to the point, he cannot die. His symbolic existence is the timeless unity of the kingdom. For example, there's no expiry date on the UK. This very idea – of a physical end to the UK – involves a category mistake. Certainly, the territory of the UK has changed over time. So have its laws and institutions and everything else that is part of it. But it is not a perishable item. It is timeless. The symbolic body of the king (an invention of English jurists in the sixteenth century), as opposed to his natural body, is always good, knowing and powerful. It shares in the attributes of the divinity (omnibenevolent, omniscient, omnipotent). The king's power is conspicuous in spectacles of public torture, as Foucault shows in the opening pages of *Discipline and Punish* with his description of Damien. The criminal is by definition someone who has made an attempt on majesty. Public torture like quartering and execution are ways for the king to display his absolute might.

Paradoxically, in spite of its timelessness, the symbolic body of the king can die. Let us consider what that means. Obviously, it doesn't mean that the present king of England falls ill and dies. It coincides with the destruction of the unity of the kingdom, not with the destruction of a land mass but with the thing that makes the UK the kingdom it is. What is that? The signifier. What does the destruction of the signifier look like? It is not the death of everyone who identify as 'English', 'Scots', 'Welsh' or who is a UK citizen by law. We have to suppose that the signifier 'United Kingdom' is destroyed without a trace. Let us say that no one recalls hearing the expression and that there are no institutions, rituals and a tradition referring to itself with that name or associated names. There is no quilting-point or master signifier signifying the whole – a nation, a kingdom and people identifying as such. What is missing is the *symbolic framework* under which events are registered oppositionally as 'UK' and 'not-UK'. The destruction of a symbolic framework is an infinitely more serious affair than the death of the person who temporarily occupies the seat of king. Without it, the subject lacks the wherewithal to understand who and where he is and what is happening.

Or consider the following reflections. It is certain that I will die at some point in time. I don't know when but I know that I will. Moreover, I occupy various symbolic positions. I am a professor at university, a father of two, a lover to a friend and so on. It is likely that some of these symbolic positions will survive my death. I will not cease to be a father to my children, for instance. As for my institutional position, its status will change, of course, but it won't get erased from the record. I will live on in the institutional memory for as long as the institution exists. Conversely, suppose I legally disown my children. My symbolic position as father will cease before my physical existence expires. All this shows that my symbolic and physical existence don't coincide.

Žižek considers the following two cases to illustrate the point. Antigone in Sophocles' eponymous play suffers a symbolic death before she physically dies. She is ostracized and a criminal according to her uncle Creon's edict, 'Traitors of Thebes are not to be given the customary burial rights.' She buries her brother Polynices, a traitor, nonetheless. Her action does not issue from her symbolic position as a member of Thebes and of its royal family. On the contrary, it is her action that gets her in trouble and that causes her to lose her symbolic place. It issues from the drive (the Thing). That is what makes her sublime. Antigone disregards the differences between friend and enemy of the state – one of the political differences Creon sets great store on – as well as the moral differences between doing good and bad deeds. It doesn't matter what her brother has done. He is still her brother and he is owed the rite of burial and mourning by a family member – by, in this instance, his sister. Whatever he has done and whatever the world (the big Other) thinks of him, she loves him for who he is. Her attachment to her brother bypasses the symbolic order. It is an attachment at the level of the id or drive. That is why her love leads to her doom. This drive-attachment, which is in excess of symbolic relations and disruptive of them, is what 'imbues her character with sublime beauty' (SOI 150).

Conversely, Žižek refers to the ghost of Hamlet's father as a case where the subject continues to exist symbolically after his physical death. Hamlet's father continues to live on in Hamlet for as long as his son doesn't settle his father's account (to, notably, avenge his death), which leads to Hamlet's doom.

A subject whose symbolic existence is unaccompanied by his physical existence tends to take on a spectral or monstrous appearance, whereas a subject whose physical existence is unaccompanied by a symbolic existence or place in the world has the tendency to appear sublime and exercises fascination on the mind, being at once an object of attraction and repulsion. It is as if the Real were right before our eyes.

It is symbolic death that interests Žižek in the chapter. Symbolization entails its opposite that limits it, the unsymbolizable. It is part of its own immanent unfolding that it should hit upon a traumatic limit for which the signifier is inadequate and lacking. Symbolization finds its limit in the drive. The drive is included in the symbolic order as its outermost limit, as the point at which it breaks down. Žižek speaks of an 'empty place' in the symbolic order. Human '*history* differs from animal *evolution* precisely by its reference to this *non-historical* place, a place which cannot be symbolized, although it is produced retroactively by the symbolization itself: as soon as "brute", pre-symbolic reality is symbolized/historicized, it "secretes", it isolates the empty, "indigestible" place of the Thing' (SOI 150). The drive is the tension that remains 'after' the symbolization of empirical reality. It is what the subject cannot work off. Let me make explicit what remains implicit in Žižek's claim:

(a) *History* and the *symbolization of empirical reality* are the same. What is symbolized becomes by that fact part of history, that is, it becomes historical. Even nature is historical in this sense – nature as the object of modern science. For what founds modern science is Galileo's mathematization of nature, the claim that nature speaks the language of mathematics.

(b) What exceeds symbolization exceeds by that fact the difference between nature and history and, generally speaking, oppositionality, it being the formal feature of the symbolic. The drive is non-historical and yet, it is not part of nature; it is not instinct. The *other* of the symbolic order is part of neither history nor nature. It doesn't belong *within the constituted domains* of the symbolic order. It is the unthinkable-impossible-unsayable that nevertheless happens.

At stake is the Thing, which is neither a signifier nor an imagined object nor something empirically real, yet it at the same time produces effects and endures as a traumatism. It 'enables us to conceive the possibility of a total, global annihilation of the signifier's network' (SOI 150). Or again: "absolute death, the 'destruction of the universe", is always the destruction of the *symbolic* universe' (SOI 151). The death drive involves destruction not because 'death' is its aim, but because it is an intensity whose increase explodes the unity of the signifier.

Benjamin's 'Theses on the Philosophy of History'

Žižek turns to Benjamin's *Theses on the Philosophy of History* because it approaches the death drive (unwittingly) as the 'degree zero' of history. Benjamin thinks of history as Lacan thinks of a text, as, notably, a series of events whose meaning is produced retroactively.

Benjamin's first thesis is paradoxical. It states that historical materialism can triumph only with the aid of theology – that is, with the very thing Marx rejects as ideological. The allegory of Thesis I is as follows. A puppet is sitting at a chess table and wins every time against its opponent. A hunchback is hidden in the table – no one sees him because of the way the mirrors are arranged – causing the puppet to move the pieces. The puppet is historical materialism, the hunchback and master chess player is theology.[1]

Let's first get a grip on the ordinary sense of these terms:

- Historical materialism is Marx's thesis that history is governed by causal laws and that any kind of social conflict is reducible to and can be explained by the class conflict. It is a *materialist* theory in the sense that the *economic base* of society has an ultimate causal-explanatory power.
- Theology is *revealed* (God is an object of faith) or *rational* (the attributes of God are known through reason), it is supernatural or natural.

If you use theology to account for what happens in the world, then you're a spiritualist rather than a materialist. God has an ultimate causal-explanatory power. It accounts for whatever happens in the universe, indeed, for its very existence. There is no doubt that Benjamin's thesis is meant to shock the reader. However, it is also clear that he isn't using 'theology' and 'historical materialism' in their ordinary meanings. What, then, does 'theology' mean in his text? It qualifies a certain experience of history, one that is antithetical to the way the victors experience it. Benjamin's victors experience history in two connected ways:

- History is a progress that terminates with the ones in power. (Benjamin is the first to link progress to domination. An example of it is Francis

Fukuyama's bastardized version of Hegel's the 'end of history' thesis. For Fukuyama, history comes to an end at the end of the cold war. It comes to an end with the unopposed and unstoppable expansion of liberalism and capitalism.)

- The victor's historian construes history as a homogeneous continuum. History has the form of the consecutive order of time. It is a universal framework, that is, one that is the same for everyone.

If that is how the victors write history, 'theology' names a different experience and approach. 'What Benjamin has in mind is, on the contrary, the *isolation* of a piece of the past from the continuity of history' (SOI 153). In other words, Benjamin's historian – his historical materialist – looks for the *failed* moments of the past, the revolutionary action that failed or was forgotten or repressed by those who won. Why? Because they bear the promise of change and of the redemption of the past. The question of justice guides Benjamin's theological view of history.

For Benjamin, it is not a question of situating the past and understanding it in context. History is not a science. There is no objective view of the past. There is the past of the victors and there is the past of those who lost, the downtrodden, and there is no common measure between them. What exists between them is a relation of domination. Thesis VI: 'To articulate the past historically does not mean to recognize it "the way it really was."'[2] Thesis XII: 'Not man or men but the struggling, oppressed class itself is the depository of historical knowledge.'[3] This is a standard Marxist claim. The oppressed have an insight into the mechanisms of oppression, not in fact but in principle, and it is a matter of occupying their standpoint to understand how they work. It's a normative question, one that concerns truth. But that is not what Benjamin has in mind.

History can be written in two ways. You can write it from the standpoint of the victors and from that of the vanquished. In the former perspective, time is understood (a) as a homogenous medium and (b) as involving a progression from an earlier to a later state posited as its goal – as, indeed, the meaning of the entire course. The historian here 'sees history as a closed continuity of "progression" leading to the reign of those who rule today. It leaves out of consideration what *failed* in history, what has to be denied so that the continuity of 'what really happened' could establish itself' (SOI 154).

For the historical materialist, on the other hand, 'History is the subject of a structure whose site is not homogeneous, empty time but time filled with by the presence of the now (*Jetztzeit*)' (Thesis XIV). Benjamin gives the following as an example of time filled by the now:

> Thus, to Robespierre ancient Rome was a past charged with the time of the now which he blasted out of the continuum of history. The French revolution viewed itself as Rome reincarnate. It evoked ancient Rome the way fashion evokes costumes of the past.[4]

The *failed* past reactivated by the French Revolution in the eyes of Robespierre was Republican Rome, the Rome of Cicero, not the Rome of the Caesars, of, say, Seneca. In this connection, that is, in connection with the hundreds of thousands in France brought to the point of starvation, Žižek says that 'the oppressed class appropriates the past to itself in so far as it is "open", in so far as the "yearning for redemption" is already at work in it – that is to say, it appropriates the past insofar as the past already contains – in the form of what failed, of what was extirpated – the dimension of the future' (SOI 154). For the historical materialist, *the past is a vehicle for revolutionary action*; and isn't the purpose of revolution to redeem injustices? Thesis II: 'The past carries with it a temporal index by which it is referred to redemption.'[5]

For the historical materialist, the present is not a transition. It is a moment in which time stands still. The now (*Jetztzeit*) blasts open the historiographer's homogeneous temporal framework. Benjamin says the same thing about thinking. Thesis XVII: thinking involves not only a flow of thoughts,

> but their arrest as well. Where thinking suddenly stops in a configuration pregnant with tensions, it gives that configuration a shock, by which it crystallizes into a monad. A historical materialist approaches a historical subject only when he encounters it as a monad. In this structure he recognizes the sign of a Messianic cessation of happening [of history in the ordinary sense], or, put differently, a revolutionary chance in the fight for the oppressed past.[6]

Let me highlight several points in the passage:

- A monad. For Leibniz, it is a metaphysical point, an active living (and, in the case of humans, also a mental) substance comprising an endless flow of representations and appetites. A monad is a point of view on the universe that is incommensurable with that of other monads (monads are individuated inwardly by their representational and appetitive contents). In other words, it is a discrete living substance that represents the universe from an irreplaceable point of view. Benjamin is using the word metaphorically to single out the *Jetztzeit*. I suspect that he has the following in mind. A failed moment contains a representation of the world (a symbolic universe) incommensurable with the one currently in force. To reactivate it is tantamount to a revolution. In what sense is it a cessation of the flow of time? Presumably in the sense that by reactivating it, the victor's historian's temporal framework dissolves. You can identify a flow (a change) against a permanent background. The latter is the temporal framework. It is what persists through the change. If you dissolve the persisting framework, then you deprive yourself of the means by which to determine the difference between what persists and what changes. That is what Benjamin's historical materialist is after. Thesis XV:

The great revolution introduced a new calendar. The initial day of a calendar serves as a historical time-lapse camera. And, basically, it is the same day that keeps recurring in the guise of holidays, which are days of remembrance. Thus the calendars do not measure time as clocks do [i.e., clocks = homogeneous time]; they are monuments of historical consciousness of which not the slightest trace has been apparent in Europe in the past hundred years.[7]

- Time is reckoned differently with a calendar and a clock. The smallest unit of an ordinary clock – the second – is homogeneous. Every second is the same as every other. Clock-time leads to the abstract notion of homogeneous time. It leads to the victor's historian writing history in the background of a temporal framework that is the same for everyone. The days on a calendar are not all the same. There is a qualitative difference between holidays and workdays and between the holidays themselves. For Benjamin's theologian-historical materialist, what is at stake is

> locating the moments of revolutionary action that failed in the past and whose reactivation could lead to the institution of a new calendar, that is, in Lacan's terms, a new symbolic universe – in short, a different way of organizing and representing human life. This moment that blasts open the victor's historian temporal framework is Messianic. It can redeem the past, it can make whole again what was left scattered and in ruins.

In Žižek's eyes (SOI 156), what Benjamin says about the relation between the failed past excised from homogeneous time is compatible with the Freudian understanding of the repressed unconscious in relation to the system preconscious-consciousness. The repressed unconscious is *not* in time. By contrast, consciousness situates its objects in time or in reference to a fixed temporal framework. The repressed unconscious: that is, infantile impulses, that is, the pleasure-seeking impulses of infancy. They are ever-present or return compulsively in pathological behaviour, as well as in dreams, in slips of the tongue and bungled actions. Likewise the *Jetztzeit* in Benjamin. The failed past is present in homogeneous time as a symptom, that is, as its limit and possible undoing. It is the revolutionary moment on which the historical materialist sets her sight. Another way of putting the same thing:

(a) There is the past that you can remember. This is the past that you can be conscious of and that you can also forget. It's the past you've lived through and experienced first-hand. Call it the conscious past.

(b) There is the past that you cannot remember because you did not live through it. For example, your prenatal existence in the womb or the age of dinosaurs. Because such things are empirical facts, however, you can learn about them. Call it the learnt past. It is impersonal because it was not actually experienced by you. It can be forgotten in the sense that things learnt as a child usually are forgotten later in life. Such facts as my birth or the age of dinosaurs can be plotted in homogeneous time even if we follow Kant and Freud and suppose that time is a function of consciousness and that it doesn't exist without it. It is plainly wrong to believe that consciousness must have lived through the age of dinosaurs in order to know stuff about them, such as when they roamed the earth. The temporal framework, being homogeneous and uniform, is objectively valid. It holds for the past and future in general. (In effect, the fact that there is no qualitative difference between the past and future is one of its central features.) Given the availability of facts in the present and reliable dating instruments, the time of dinosaurs on earth can be dated accurately.

(c) There is finally the failed past. The analogy with the repressed unconscious in Lacan as a trace that awaits interpretation from the future is apt. The idea is not that what doesn't happen leaves behind an unconscious trace. Instead, we must understand by 'failure' not what doesn't happen but what resists symbolization, what is traumatic or too much, too intense to be registered in a symbolic framework. Call it the repressed past. It is possible to say that it 'endures' outside of chronological time insofar as it resists entry into the symbolic order – in other words, insofar as it lacks a signified-meaning. It endures alongside the continuity of time as a virtuality or symptom.

Žižek says the following about the reactivation of the repressed past.

> The monad is thus the moment of discontinuity, of rupture, at which the linear 'flow of time' is suspended, arrested, 'coagulated', because in it resounds directly – that is to say: bypassing the linear succession of continuous time – the past which was repressed, pushed out of the continuity established by prevailing history. (SOI 157)

Take an emancipatory struggle. Its adherents find that it echoes past failed struggles, that they repeat themselves in it (like a symptom) with the future they bore. The 'now' that blasts open the continuity of homogeneous time brings history back to its degree zero by making possible another history, that of the formerly vanquished. It makes it possible to retrieve the past failed struggles and retroactively determine their meaning and thus redeem them.

> the actual revolutionary situation presents an attempt to 'unfold' the symptom, to 'redeem' – that is, to realize in the Symbolic – these past failed attempts which 'will have been' only through their repetition, at which point they become retroactively what they already were (SOI 158; see also SE 319).

It is now clear in light of what oppositions Žižek frames his reading of Benjamin. The Real and the Symbolic correspond, in Benjamin's text, to the monad or *Jetztzeit* and homogeneous time, or, what is the same, to the difference between the vanquished and the victor. The vanquished at the edge of the symbolic order are coextensive with the Real. History as it is experienced by them is not linear. It is a constellation in which there coexists the present and the repressed pasts with which it resonates. The time of the now (*Jetztzeit*) is a structure 'shot through with chips of Messianic time'.[8]

The retroactive constitution of meaning – Lacan's idea that an event's meaning is determined by the future – taken to the extreme entails the idea of the Last Judgement, that is, the point of view at the end of time from where everything that has taken place in history is finally determined in its significance – the point at which the totality of history is summed up and its parts are assigned their definitive place in it. 'Actual history occurs, so to speak, on credit' (SOI 159). If the future decides what the past will have meant, then the meaning of the past will finally come to light at the end of time. Žižek claims that this notion is at work in Stalin's account of history, which at bottom amounts to the idea that the end justifies the means: it is morally OK to put innocent victims on trial as long as subsequent social progress justifies it. For Benjamin, this theological perspective of the end of time belongs to the vanquished. It is the 'perspective of hopes deceived, of all that have left in the text of history nothing but scattered, anonymous, meaningless traces on the margin of deeds whose "historical greatness" was attested to by the "objective gaze" of official historiography' (SOI 161).

Žižek distinguishes between two positions in the background of his comparison of Benjamin and Stalin:

- Evolutionary idealism. It is the position of the victor. It is the view that history is a teleological progress. It is idealistic because what causes progress is an immaterial property, the goal.
- Materialist creationist. It is the position of the historical materialist. It is the view that the future is *ex nihilo*. It is without precedent in the past. It arises from nothing and it is, therefore, absolutely new. By reactivating the repressed past, Benjamin's historical materialist owes nothing to the history

of the victors. On the contrary, his reactivation abolishes their symbolic-temporal framework and, *for this reason*, what he does issues from the drive (the Real). In this way, too, is every failed past redeemed – every repressed past that echoes with the 'now' excised from homogenous time. It is a materialist view not because it takes economic activities or the class conflict as basic, but because it is grounded in the Real of the drive.

Power and its representation

At the end of the Chapter, Žižek distinguishes between the classical master, e.g., the king, the totalitarian leader, for example, Stalin, and the democratic notion of the People. This distinction is drawn from the point of view of the sublime body that survives the physical death of the leader or master.

(a) Let us recall that the sublime body of the king represents the timeless unity of the kingdom. His symbolic body is the effect of certain rituals and performatives. We, 'the subjects, think that we treat the king as a king because he is in himself a king, but in reality the king is a king because we treat him like one. And this fact that the charismatic power of the king is an effect of the symbolic ritual performed by his subjects must remain hidden' (SOI 163). The illusion we fall prey to is that the king is king by nature. We don't recognize the fact that he is king because that is how we treat him. When the illusion fails, however, it is not the case that we then recognize that the king was always naked beneath his clothes. The king begins to legitimize his rule by some extra-symbolic standard: Nature, God, the mythical past and so on.

(b) The totalitarian leader says to the people that in himself he is nothing. He is all in all their representative. Where does the illusion lie here? He suspends the illusion at work in the relation of subjects to their king. He makes explicit what remains implicit in aristocracy – that the king rules only so long as they treat him as their king. The illusion here lies in the tautological definition of the People. The Leader and the Party legitimize their rule by reference to the real interests of the People, while the interests of the People are made to coincide with the interests of the Leader and Party. To go against the Party is to go against the interests of the People. Who are the People? Well, the Party and its Leader . . . 'That is why the real member of the People is only he who supports the rule of the Party: those who work against its rule are automatically excluded from the People; they become "the enemies of the People"' (SOI 165).

(c) In a democracy, the People are sovereign and the place of the People – the locus of power or sovereignty – is temporarily occupied by the winning majority, which is to say that in principle, it remains vacant. The place of power is left empty in a democracy. The People (the symbolic order) cannot be embodied in a representative once and for all without reverting back to an aristocratic or totalitarian mode. Lefort's claim that the place of power is left empty in a democracy means that society doesn't exist, that it is not a fact but a representation, and that there are competing representations and that they are one and all incommensurable with one another.

Žižek turns to Lefort at the end of the chapter in order to show an alternative way in which the Real intervenes and upends the symbolic order (ideology), that is, different from the revolutionary action of Benjamin's historical materialist. For Lefort, the Real irrupts at elections. An election dissolves the People into a plurality of formal quantitative units. Every person counts as one regardless of who he or she is, of his or her station in life and achievements and wealth. In a formal democracy,

> we take part as abstract citizens, atomized individuals, reduced to pure Ones without further qualifications. At the moment of elections, the *whole hierarchic network of social relations* [my emphasis] is in a way suspended, put in parenthesis; 'society' as an organic unity ceases to exist, it changes into a contingent collection of atomized individuals, abstract units, and the result depends upon a purely quantitative mechanism of counting, ultimately on a stochastic process: some wholly unforeseeable event – a

> scandal which erupts a few days before election, for example – can add that 'half percent' one way or the other that determines the general orientation of the country's politics over the next few years. (SOI 166)

Democracy is made possible by giving oneself over to this risk. To eliminate it together with the possibility of manipulation is to eliminate the possibility of democracy.

Study questions

1. Explain the difference between symbolic and physical death?
2. Why is Benjamin's 'Theses on the Philosophy of History' important for Žižek?

Section 5

Chapter 5 of *The Sublime Object of Ideology* adds to the earlier Chapters on the ideological constitution of the subject. Its focus is on the Real and the kind of objects that embody it. One of the central claims of the Chapter is that what it repudiates (the Real) sustains the subject's coherence and identity.

'There is no metalanguage': Derrida and dissemination

Is Lacan a post-structuralist? That is the question of the first ten pages of the Chapter. At the same time, 'post-structuralism' is code for Derrida and deconstruction and the first third of the chapter reads as a defence of Lacan against Derrida's critique in 'Le facteur de la vérité' in *The Post-Card: From Socrates to Freud and Beyond*. Žižek continues his defence of Lacan against Derrida two years later in Chapter 1 of ES.

In *The Sublime Object of Ideology*, Žižek approaches the matter from the point of view of Lacan's statement in Seminar 12, *Crucial Problems for Psychoanalysis*, that there is no metalanguage. The latter involves the idea that we use words to talk about words and not only about (nonverbal) things. For example, '"Voiture" is the French for car'. 'Car' in the sentence is the metalinguistic term, it is the term used to refer not to an object in the world but to a word in another language, French. The cited 'voiture' is part of the object language. According to Alfred Tarski, we must distinguish between the following:

1. The object language. This is the language whose syntactic and semantic features are being studied. By putting its sentences in quotation

marks, we suspend their reference so that their properties can become thematic. Any language, both natural and formal, can become an object language.

2. The metalanguage. This is the language used to determine the truth conditions of the object language.

Tarski develops this distinction in order to resolve paradoxes like 'I am lying' or 'This sentence is false.' The paradox is evident. If 'I am lying' is true then it is false (because I am lying). The proposition is both true and false at the same time. The paradox disappears by insisting that 'truth' is not a predicate of the object language but of the metalanguage. To use the classical example, '"Snow is white" is true iff snow is white.'

The quoted sentence on the left 'Snow is white' is part of the object language. Its truth condition is determined by the conditional 'iff snow is white' in the metalanguage. Paradoxes like 'I am lying' are sidestepped in this way.

'I am lying' is true iff *p*.

There is nothing contradictory in saying that 'I am lying' is true if *p*-conditions are met. Tarski short-circuits paradoxes of this sort by insisting that no language is 'semantically closed', that is, no language can contain its own truth-predicate.

In literary theory, the distinction is cashed out as follows:

1. The novel or poem.
2. The commentary on the novel or poem.

The post-structuralist claim is that *1 and 2 cannot be distinguished or separated, neither in the novel or poem nor in the commentary*. Every literary work includes a commentary on itself. It contains an account of the conditions that make it possible. Conversely, there is no commentary that is so 'theoretical' that it doesn't involve literary tropes or linguistic devices standardly used in literary works. The claim is thus the following:

- It is not possible to draw, within a given text or language, whether natural or formal, literary or philosophical, an unequivocal distinction between the object language and metalanguage. There is, instead, a continuity between the one and the other.

Žižek writes:

> Thus the interpretation is included in the literary corpus: there is no 'pure' literary object that would not contain an element of interpretation, of distance towards its immediate meaning. In post-structuralism the classic opposition between the object-text and its external interpretative reading is thus replaced by a continuity of an infinite literary text which is always already its own reading. (SOI 171)

The 'post-structuralist' procedure is typically twofold: (a) it identifies, in the literary work, the ensemble of propositions that account for how it works or the literary effects it produces; (b) it shows that even 'high theory' is indistinguishable from 'literature' in a broad sense. The latter claim entails, as a corollary, putting in parenthesis the text's claim to being true and show how it brings it about. Suppose I read the *New Testament* and it strikes me as being in agreement with reality. Suppose further that everything it says is actually false. It follows that unless there is something seriously wrong with me, the text is using rhetorical devices to produce this truth effect. Finally, it stands to reason that this is true of every text, including those that are correct.

Before exploring Žižek's response to Derrida's criticism of Lacan – that Lacan attempts to limit the dissemination of language by localizing lack in a signifier, the phallus – let me set the context. Allow me to explain, in brief, what dissemination amounts to. Deconstruction shows that no text is safe from it. Signifiers are joined in paratactic and hypotactic structures. They form patterns. There is no end to this process because the signified is lacking that would tie up the signifiers in a closed system.

Žižek is right to emphasize that Derrida privileges paratactic over hypotactic connections, metonymic associations over metaphorical ones. The element of chance is more emphatically conspicuous in linguistic constructions of this type than in combinations having a metaphorical pattern. Metonymic associations are representative of the id (the death drive), metaphoric ones of the ego. The former relate to part-objects, the latter to whole-objects.

Dissemination for Derrida also relates to the thought that Žižek himself develops in Chapter 4 of *The Sublime Object of Ideology* in his reading of Lacan. This is that language relates to a constitutive outside, to, notably, the remainderless destruction of the symbolic order. A signifier is a relation to another signifier, yes, it signifies it as its signified, which signifies another as its signified and so on. But a signifier also relates to what lacks a signified, that is to say, to the possibility of its impossibility (the Real). This usually transpires in Derrida's reflections on the apocalyptic end of the world and the Other (the infinite) in Levinas. We might think of it as follows. The symbolic order is structured around a central impossibility, that is, the impossibility of marking the limit of language. It's like saying that you cannot understand madness from *its* point of view because it has none, but only from the point of view reason. What madness is in itself is impossible to say. And yet, that central impossibility is just what reason gravitates around because it is its traumatizing limit and undoing. The signifier of this limit – of the limit of language, of reason, its outside – is missing. (It goes without saying that this 'outside' is not the empirical world, for the latter is penetrated by the signifier.) And so every signifier in the structure can be read as supplementing, or making up for, this missing signifier. It's as if every signifier in the system were at bottom a stand-in for it. Now this is how language operates. Signifiers are combined with and substituted for one another and, in doing so, they mask the lack on account of which language is essentially an open and incomplete system.

Derrida's criticism as Žižek reads it targets the notion of the phallus in Lacan.

> Post-structuralists see the Lacanian theory of the *point de capiton*, of the phallic signifier as the signifier of lack, as an effort to master and restrain the 'dissemination' of the textual process. Is it not, they say, an attempt to localize a lack in a single signifier, the One, although it is the signifier of lack? Derrida repeatedly reproaches Lacan for the paradoxical gesture of reducing lack through its affirmation of itself. Lack is localized in a point of exception which guarantees the consistency of all the other elements, by the mere fact that it is determined as 'symbolic castration', by the mere fact that the phallus is defined as its signifier. (172-173)

Žižek is saying that Derrida challenges the privilege Lacan assigns to the phallus. The phallus is the signifier of meaning in general and of what the Other desires. It behaves as the thing for whose absence it makes up. It behaves as a foundation or signified. It renders a text stable and consistent, giving it temporary closure. Derrida knows that Lacan's psychoanalysis is designed to expose this phallic pretence. He knows that it unmasks its phallic function by showing it to be a contingent element and that the symbolic order is structurally inconsistent. Nevertheless, according to Žižek, Derrida challenges the idea that it is possible to localize the lack inherent to language in a privileged signifier. At bottom, there is no privileged signifier – not of lack, not of anything else. I think Derrida is right about this. The fact that Žižek doesn't respond to this challenge could mean that he concedes Derrida's point.

Žižek claims that Derrida is being inconsistent, however. On his reading, there is for Derrida (as there is for post-structuralism) a continuity between the object language and metalanguage. Yet Derrida occupies a metalinguistic position 'in its purest, most radical form' (SOI 173) when he asserts that, for example, there is no text that fully escapes the metaphysics of presence. Žižek's suspicion is that Derrida's position can be stated in a few theoretical propositions, that is, independently of the literary devices he couches them in. I doubt that Derrida would deny this. There are interviews where Derrida formulates, in several central propositions, the fundamental insights of deconstruction. In some of his early interviews in *Points... Interviews, 1974–94*, he states clearly what deconstruction is and how it proceeds without recourse to literary tropes. This is not to say that Žižek is right. On the contrary, his criticism does not hit the mark. Deconstruction is not a theory, it is the inner movement of a text, of, that is, language. Oppositional terms are formed and destabilized by an unaccounted-for and surprising third term. This movement can be traced in any text providing certain strategies of reading are in place. It is possible to understand in a few propositions how a car moves, but that doesn't substitute for seeing it move on the streets. The same is true of deconstruction. It is possible to understand how it works in a few propositions. But seeing it work in a text, in Plato's or Rousseau's, is a different kind of thing altogether.

Žižek's remarks on Derrida are brief, they are too quickly dismissive and overly general to provide the reader a *point d'appui* for a proper critical response.

Lacan and 'Lenin in Warsaw'

What, then, does Lacan mean when he says that 'there is no metalanguage'? He means that it is a position impossible to occupy. Žižek draws on Brecht to give the following as an example. An actor enters on stage. He says that he is a capitalist and that his aim is to exploit his workers and that he will try to convince them of the truth of bourgeois ideology. And so he does. Naturally, his position is absurd. His commentary on his action is self-defeating. Telling his workers that he is going to exploit them obviously precludes him from being able to exploit them. He must keep his workers in the dark about the meaning of his action. By commenting on it, he makes it impossible to carry out his proposed plan. In that sense, a metalinguistic position is impossible.

Žižek associates metalanguage with the Real in Lacan on the ground that it is paradoxically a position one cannot avoid and that one cannot attain. It is impossible to occupy it, yet 'it is even more difficult simply to *avoid* it. One cannot *attain* it, but one also cannot *escape* it. That is why the only way to avoid the Real is to produce an utterance of pure metalanguage which, by its patent absurdity, materializes its own impossibility'. Žižek's point is that the Real (the lack) must be instituted in a signifier. Without it, it is not possible to sustain 'the radical dimension of the gap'. (SOI 175)

The paradox attaching to the phallus in Lacan is that it signifies the very opposite of what it usually means. It is ordinarily taken to mean the male genital organ and what the latter signifies in its erect disposition: potency, plenitude, power. In Lacan, the phallus is the signifier of castration, of, precisely, the missing foundation. How does it entail the impossibility of metalanguage? Žižek suggests that we read Lacan's claim that 'there is no metalanguage' literally as saying that there is only an object language. The object in question is not the empirical world but *objet a*, the thing the subject's renounced on entering language and that it seeks to recover with the medium of the signifier. There is no metalanguage, that is, language turns on the lacking *objet a* even when words are used to speak of words. The '*objet petit a*, as the original lost object which in a way coincides with its own loss, is precisely the embodiment of this loss' (SOI 178).

The joke he uses to illustrate it makes the point very well. There is a picture called 'Lenin in Warsaw' that depicts Lenin's wife having sex with a young man. The visitor looking at the picture asks 'But where is Lenin?'. The guide says 'Lenin is in Warsaw.' The visitor misunderstands the title. He takes it as a commentary on the picture when it is a part of it. The title names the object missing from the picture, the *objet a*, that anchors its meaning and interpretation. The 'metalanguage' – the commentary – is part of the object language and what it refers to is the phallic signifier, the thing missing from the object language (the absent Lenin) that gives it (the picture) its coherence. 'Here the title is, so to speak, on the same surface. It is part of the same continuity as the picture itself. Its distance from the picture is strictly internal, making an incision into the picture' (SOI 179). The title of the picture is a signifier that substitutes for the thing missing in it and that makes its interpretation coherent. Now isn't that precisely what Derrida objects to, the fact that, thanks to the missing thing its title names, the picture can be read so well?

The Real revisited

In the last section, we saw how an object that is absent from the picture organizes the picture's meaning and reading. The title 'Lenin in Warsaw' isn't a commentary on the picture but a part of it and, as such, an instance of the Real: Lenin's absence is the point around which the picture takes on a definite meaning. In the following two sections, Žižek explores different senses of the 'Real' in Lacan. Note that we are still dealing with the same question as before. We are dealing with the advent of the subject of the unconscious. In what sense? The 'Real' is a term that stands for the drive and separation from it, that is, the distance established by the symbolic order, is the condition *sine qua non* for the subject to arise. The 'Real' is used to mean sometimes all, sometimes some and sometimes one of the following:

1. The drive
2. The maternal Thing

3. The *objet a*, which is a representative (*Vorstellungsrepräsentanz*) of the drive or maternal Thing.

In all three cases, the Real is something *lost* or *absent*. It is experienced by the subject as *a part of itself* that it's had to sacrifice in order to enter the symbolic order and acquire a position of its own in relation to the Other's desire. Proximity to it – that is, to maternal enjoyment (*jouissance*) – produces anxiety and traumatizes. It is not separation, it is the lack of separation that causes the subject anxiety (as Lacan shows in his reading of Little Hans) and that makes necessary the intervention of the symbolic function of the father.

We have already seen how the Real operates in ideological discourse. The antagonism inherent to language becomes, by means of fantasy, an empirical obstacle localized in the Other. The Real is that part of the subject alienated in the Other that causes him to love or hate her. In either case, it is the reason why the subject is not indifferent to the Other.

In Lacan's work in the 1950s, the 'Real' is the *pre-symbolic reality* of the body as continuous and lacking nothing. It seems close to the pantheistic 'all'. Beyond or outside of empirical reality with its discrete objects in space and time – in the way, in other words, empirical reality is articulated by the signifier – there is an undivided continuity, a mutual penetration of things, an unbroken fullness. I'm thinking, for instance, of Anaxagoras' 'all is in all', and, closer to home, of Bataille's continuity in *Erotism* and the *Theory of Religion*.

In the 1970s, the 'Real' has the sense of a construct. It is an unconscious fantasy reconstructed during analysis to account for structural phenomena and pathological disorders exhibited by the patient, stuff like repetitions, displacements and so on.

> The Real is an entity which must be constructed afterwards so that we can account for the distortions of the symbolic structure. (SOI 182)

I have dealt with two instances of it in Section 2, the parricide of the primal father in Freud's *Totem and Taboo* and the second version of the fantasy in 'A Child is Being Beaten' where the patient imagines herself being beaten by her father. The following remarks should also shed some light. Take a trauma like being sexually abused as a child. The question should not be, at least in the first instance, whether the abuse took place but what kind of effects it has had on the subject. Freud abandoned his early theory of the parental seduction of the child because he could not believe that abuse was as frequent and widespread as his female patients complained. What he did not realize at the time is that the unconscious doesn't discriminate between reality and fantasy and that an unconscious fantasy of seduction is as traumatic as actual abuse in life. In effect, as we know, the abuse in life does not become traumatic until it is internalized and relived as a memory or fantasy. It is the memory or fantasy coupled with the mature understanding of what transpired in early childhood that brings on the trauma. Prior to that, there is no trauma. Seduction, in short, is a primal fantasy, as is the primal scene (parental coitus as the scene of the subject's creation) and castration (entrance into the symbolic order through the loss of the Real). These fantasies are unconscious and are the sources of various pathological disturbances. Žižek says of the primal parricide that 'it would be senseless to search for its traces in prehistoric reality, but it must nonetheless be presupposed if we want to account for the present state of things' (SOI 182–183). He adds the following:

> The paradox of the Lacanian Real, then, is that it is an entity which, although it does not exist (in the sense of 'really exist', taking place in reality), has a series of properties – it exercises a certain structural causality, it can produce a series of effects in the symbolic reality of subjects. (SOI 183)

The Real doesn't exist. What does that mean? Empirical reality is symbolically articulated. The Real is the limit of the symbolic order and, by extension, of the empirical world. It cannot be signified. 'Existence,' or, more precisely, the difference between what is present and absent and, beyond that, between being and nonbeing, is a function of the signifier. Yet what lacks a signifier can have a much more profound and traumatizing effect than what exists and can be spoken of and understood. After talking about the McGuffin in Hitchcock, Žižek adds that 'That would be, then, the precise definition of the real object: a cause which in itself does not exist – which is present only in a series of effects, but always in a distorted, displaced way' (SOI 184).

To see this from another angle, let us suppose for a moment that the Real is the foundation of the symbolic order. It is the first term in the chain of signifiers and it is possible to derive them from it; or, what amounts to the same thing, it is the last term in the chain in which they find their meaning. Now the fact is that there is neither a first nor a last term in language considered as a structure. There is, instead, a void (the Real). And, far from it having no effects, the chain of signifiers gravitates around it: they displace or metaphorize it. The lack is the Real and it is a structural feature of the symbolic on account of which it is constitutively open and incomplete.

Another way of putting this is to say that the signifier of this hole (the phallus) is the memorial of the subject's castration, of what it's had to sacrifice in order to become a subject with a desire of its own. Of course, the subject has in truth never had to part with a part of itself. The symbolization of empirical reality has this retroactive effect on the subject. It produces the feeling that something is lacking in life, something that the subject cannot quite put its finger on, a lack it thinks can be quelled. This is what is sometimes meant by 'enjoyment' (*jouissance*), and Žižek accordingly identifies it with the Real. The 'Real par excellence is *jouissance*: *jouissance* does not exist, it is impossible, but it produces a number of traumatic effects' (SOI 184). Enjoyment is the satisfaction obtained by the drive. Recall that the fundamental conflict staged by psychoanalysis is that between the ego and the id. The interests of the two do not align. What the drive demands brings about an increase of tension in the organism. It is in contradiction with the welfare of the living being (the ego).

Freedom and the forced choice: the Real

Žižek's discussion of the forced choice in Lacan adds to the notion of the Real and to his treatment of ideology. In Seminar 11 *The Four Fundamental Concepts of Psychoanalysis*, Lacan says that entering society depends on a forced choice, on the same kind of choice the street mugger visits on his victim: 'Your money or your life?' If you choose your money, then you lose both your money and your life. If you choose your life, then you lose your money. The point is that you are not given a real choice. Either you lose big or you lose small. In both cases, you lose something. That is what psychoanalysis teaches us. To enter society is to sacrifice a part of yourself. It is to give something up. As I explained earlier, however, the subject doesn't actually renounce something. The point I want to insist on is that society demands of its members to freely choose what is given to them anyway: I have not chosen the country I was born into, but I have a duty to love it and embrace its laws – or else it's a fine or prison or worse. We have a forced choice, one that performs a trick on the mind almost as powerful as witnessing water turning into wine: the forced choice turns what is almost an accident of nature (the fact that I was born here) into the product of my choosing. I am obliged to take what is *given* as though it were something *posited*, '*he must choose what is already given to him*' (SOI 186). The retroactive effect of socialization is the belief that one has freely chosen to enter society. The subject is always treated '*as if he had already chosen*' (SOI 186). Falling in love has the same effect. Let me illustrate this with Summerset Maugham's amusing short story *A Marriage of Convenience*. The man in the story is told by his superior that he will be given the job of governor of one of the French colonies on condition that he finds a wife within a month. He posts an ad in the newspaper and receives over four thousand letters in response from women from all walks of life. The man wonders how he will find the woman he is destined to be with amidst all these letters. Most of us believe that one could not fall in love except with a person of one's choosing. The intuition is that an arranged marriage is one where love is the exception rather than the rule. How could you possibly fall in love with a person you've been forced to be with by your parents or family? Nothing reinforces the point more strongly than dating apps like Tinder. The man in the story has as many options to choose from as the dating app user. We believe that it's an essential ingredient of love to freely choose to be with the person we are with. And yet, nothing seems more opposed to our idea of falling in love! Who doesn't know the following kind of story? A young man and woman meet quite by accident on the streets or in a café or restaurant. They start a conversation and end up spending the day together getting to know each other. A bond spontaneously develops. An intimacy arises. It's as if they are the only two people in the world. It's now evening. He walks her back to her apartment. They kiss in front of her door. A few months later (let us suppose) they are married. What started out by chance becomes in time something very different. They feel as if they had been destined to be together, as if their encounter was neither the product of chance nor the result of a free choice, but a preordained necessity, fate. This is what the ideological effect consists of. It modifies the modality of things: what is contingent is made to appear necessary; what is necessary is made to look like the product of a free choice; what is given appears to the subject to be posited and so on. Žižek frames the paradox of love differently than I have. For him, love is a free choice, yet a choice that never arises in the present, 'it is always already made. At a certain moment, I can only state retroactively that *I've already chosen*' (SOI 187). It is a choice made in an immemorial anteriority or before the existence of time.

Two examples. First, evil in Kant. We have contradictory beliefs about evil as we do about love. On the one hand, the intuition is that a man is evil owing to his nature and not only owing to the accidental circumstances of his birth and social environment. If someone is truly wicked, that cannot be by chance. On the contrary, it must be part of his 'eternal nature'. The suspicion is that it is possible to detect its roots and see it grow from the man's childhood onwards. At the same time and on the other hand, the intuition is that an evil man is responsible for who is and what he does. His wickedness is the result of a free choice.

> Kant's solution consists in conceiving the choice of Evil, as an atemporal, a priori, transcendental act: as an act which never took place in temporal reality but nonetheless constitutes the very frame of the subject's development, of his practical activity. (SOI 187)

Kant discusses evil in *Religion within the Bounds of Mere Reason*. His claim is that radical evil, though a predisposition, is a choice. It consists in the tendency to subordinate the moral Law to self-interest (self-love). It is not by accident that the moral Law becomes a means to the subject's welfare. It is as a result of a choice. You choose to place the one above the other. But it is a choice that paradoxically cannot be localized in time. If an act is free, then it is without antecedent causes. It is a product, not of nature, but of the subject's agency. It is, in short, an absolute beginning, that is, atemporal.

Second example, freedom in Schelling. Žižek draws here on a certain strategic reading. Kant's distinction between the noumenal and phenomenal – between, that is, freedom and nature (necessity) – is fleshed out against the Freudian distinction between the unconscious and consciousness. This identification is not unjustified, provided we recall that time exists as little in the unconscious as it does in the noumenon, that is, in the subject in its transcendental freedom. The significant departure this marks from Kant is that it entails an *identification of freedom with the unconscious* rather than with consciousness or self-consciousness (when for Kant self-consciousness and freedom are one and the same).

In the *Treatise of Human Freedom*, Schelling distinguishes between freedom and consciousness and, in support of his distinction, he draws on the common observation that sometimes we feel responsible and guilty for things we are not conscious of having done. It's as if we had done them in a time before time. The guilt bears witness to 'an unconscious choice, to an unconscious decision for Evil' (SOI 189). In psychoanalytic terms, it manifests an unconscious illicit wish.

> Such a free unconscious must be presupposed to account for the sentiment that we are guilty even for things which do not depend upon our conscious decision. (SOI 189)

So, as with the second fantasy in 'A Child is Being Beaten', freedom must be presupposed, it must be 'constructed', if we are to account for various ostensible facts (such as this guilt). On this basis, Žižek assimilates freedom to the traumatic Real: 'the traumatic event is ultimately just a fantasy-construct filling out a void in a symbolic structure and, as such, the retroactive effect of this structure' (SOI 191).

Žižek adds a few more oppositions in terms of which the Real is understood. Here are three pairs:

1. The Real – in this instance, the living body or drive – is the *presupposed ground* of symbolization, the very thing that on being symbolized, is drained of *jouissance*; it is, at the same time, the *inassimilable remainder* of symbolization, precisely what resists the signifier and what, as a result, limits symbolization.
2. The Real is a *plenitude*, a fullness, it lacks nothing. Lack is introduced by symbolization. At the same time, the Real is the *lack*, it is the hole that symbolization turns around. It is the effect of castration.

3. The Real is a traumatic encounter that disrupts symbolization, yet it is possible to construct it after the fact only.

Žižek writes that the Lacanian Real is 'a certain limit which is always missed' (SOI 195). Let me illustrate this with an example Lacan uses in Seminar 11 in his discussion of the repetition compulsion. He reports Freud's description in *The Interpretation of Dreams* of a man's dream who lost his son. The man's dead son is lying on a bed with a sheet over his body. An old man is keeping watch over the corpse. There is a candle by the bed. The father goes to the room next door to have a rest. He has been watching his son all day. The old man falls asleep. The candle falls on the bedsheet and causes a fire. The father keeps on dreaming of his son. His son comes up to him. He says reproachfully, 'Father, can't you see that I'm burning?'. The father is woken up by the Real, by, that is, his guilt. It interrupts his unconscious wish to continue sleeping. The guilt is the thing that he persistently misses and avoids because he cannot endure it. It's 'too much'. Generally speaking, guilt and shame are manifestations of the Real (see SOI 204).

Lack, the subject and the ontological inconsistency of the big Other

What kind of subject is compatible with the Real? The divided subject, that is, the speaking subject for which a part of it – the Real – escapes speech, that is, symbolization. Let us first remind ourselves of the subject's alienation in the signifier.

> as soon as the subject is caught in the radically external signifying network he is mortified, dismembered, divided. (SOI 196)

The signifier 'divides' the subject in at least two senses of the word:

(a) The subject has, as a result of the signifier, a *reflexive* relation to desire. It is never a matter of going after what you desire but of endorsing some and of renouncing other desires. I don't merely have desires, I relate to them. It matters to me what kind of desires I have. This is the

German Idealist insight that Žižek sometimes leans on. Nothing in the empirical world is really given to the subject as a brute fact. What is given to it is always also posited, that is, judged, evaluated, determined as so-and-so, accepted or rejected and so on.

(b) There is a difference between the speaking subject and the subject spoken of, the *sujet d'énonciation* and the *sujet d'énoncé*, the unconscious and consciousness. The latter refers to what is symbolized, to what the subject can be conscious of and talk about. The former refers to the singular and unrepeatable acts of speaking in which the subject says more than what it intends or means to say. This is where new links between signifiers are instituted and where, in consequence, unexpected effects (linguistic and non-linguistic) are produced. The unconscious is not a black box. It doesn't reside in what the subject says or wants to say. It is a performative phenomenon. It exists squarely in the *hic et nunc*.

On Žižek's reading, the 'post-structuralist' notion of the subject is an effect of pre-subjective processes. For Derrida, this is 'writing' in a broad sense where the term is equivalent to language, to its structural and temporal properties (differing/deferring). For Foucault, this is discourse and non-discursive practices, knowledge and power. For the Deleuze of *Anti-Oedipus*, this is desire. According to some of these and other authors, a human being occupies incommensurable subject-positions at different points in time. Some examples. The Enlightenment makes available a subject-position that wasn't possible in previous ages. Consider the notion of agency. It entails, among other things, that what defines me is not some empirical identity – being a member of a nation, religion or species. I am not the thing I identify with but, instead, the *act* of identifying with it. I am self-determining, a first cause of sorts, a subject that legislates to itself the norms under which it thinks and acts. In previous centuries, the human subject defines itself in reference to the whole of which it sees itself as a part: the *polis* in Greek culture, the universal brotherhood of love for the Christian, the *cosmopolis* for the Stoic and so on. What marks the onset of modernity is the recognition of the agency of the human being, the fact that it is self-defining, that it is, in other words, irreducible to the identities it possesses as a member of various groups. Or take German romanticism in the final decade of the eighteenth century. The notion of genius arises with it – in other words, the idea that the human subject, embodying the unity of art and nature or being the conduit of nature's artistic forces, is so rich in content that it explodes in multiple works. The common wisdom today derives from this romantic notion. This is that the human being is inwardly rich to such a profound extent that language isn't fine-grained enough to express everything it feels and thinks. It goes without saying that this subject-position was unavailable in prior ages. Every historical period makes available its own subject-positions. And the critical theorist's task is to account for their production by means of, for example, techniques of the self, pedagogies, regimes of truth and so on.

In contrast to this, the Lacanian subject according to Žižek comes to the foreground by stripping away, in thought, concrete historical subject-positions to the point that nothing remains save an empty place in the structure. This is the locus of the subject, the subject of the signifier. After all, it is the signifier that determines, in every case, the position and identity of the subject.

> The *subject* is therefore to be strictly opposed to the effect of *subjectivation*: what the subjectivation masks is not a pre- or trans-subjective process of writing but a lack in the structure, a lack which is the subject. (SOI 197)

'Lack' – the lack in the structure – here means lack of the maternal Thing, of *jouissance*. Castration produces the subject. It is not because it is infinitely rich on the inside that it cannot find the right words to say what it feels or thinks. It is because it is lacking that it fails to find the right signifier; 'instead of a richness we have a lack, and this void opened by the failure *is* the subject of the signifier' (SOI 198).

We can put this differently by saying that the subject's identity is a function of the Real it repudiates, that it gets its coherence from what it rejects as cause of social decay. In 'the anti-Semitic vision, the Jew is experienced as the embodiment of negativity'. The outsider is posited as the cause of the dissolution of the social harmony. The truth, of course, is that *this negative relation to the Jew* is what *sustains the identity of the social fabric*. The anti-Semitic society sustains itself on the basis of what it excludes.

> Without reference to the Jew who is corroding the social fabric, the social fabric itself would be dissolved. (SOI 199)

The identity of the anti-Semitic subject would dissolve without this negative reference to the Jew. The Jew occupies the position of the traumatic Real, of what must be excluded for the subject to achieve a minimum of coherence and self-identity. Formally expressed, what functions as the Real and occupies its position in society is, by necessity, excluded; it acts on the subject as a source of repulsion.

Another example drawn this time from Adorno. Adorno says that it is impossible to define society because we invariably end up with an irresolvable antinomy:

(a) Society is an organic whole.

(b) Society is a contract between atomized individuals.

Žižek suggests that we should look at this antinomy not as an epistemological obstacle hindering our understanding of society, but ontologically. The contradiction structures the being of society. It is impossible to define society, not because it is an unknowable thing-in-itself, but, instead, because *it is in-itself inconsistent*. The big Other is not a totality, it is in itself lacking. Lacking what? The Real. The absence of the Real in the big Other makes it ontologically inconsistent. It is why it lacks an identity of its own.

> [It] bears witness to the fact that Society itself does not exist, that it is marked by a radical impossibility. And it is because of this impossibility to achieve full identity with itself that the Other, Society as Substance, is already subject. (SOI 201) [The reference is to the Preface of Hegel's *Phenomenology of Spirit* where he says that we must think of the True not only as Substance but also as Subject.]

Žižek deepens the notion of the divided subject in the next section titled 'Subject as an "answer of the Real"' and via an examination of the notion of the question (which I do not pursue here). He says that the subject is divided 'as to the object himself, as to the Thing, which at the same time attracts and repels him' (SOI 204).

The ideological function of *objet a*

Let's recall here what the Thing and *objet a* signify. The former is the maternal body the subject is separated from owing to the paternal Law, the Name-of-the-Father or, generally speaking, the signifier. The *objet a* is what remains of the Thing after the socialization of the subject. The *objet a* is *constituted* as a lost object. It was never present, it was never possessed or enjoyed. There was never a time when the subject was whole and had to then renounce a part of itself in order to enter society. The *objet a* is a product of the Law (of separation). It is produced *retroactively* as a result of the presence of prohibitions. The subject's unconscious inference is simple and straightforward: if there are prohibitions, then I must have enjoyed pleasures that I was then forced to renounce. That is how the fantasy of fullness is produced. In *The Plague of Fantasies*, Žižek writes:

> *das Ding* is the absolute void, the lethal abyss which swallows the subject; while *objet petit a* designates that which remains of the Thing after it has undergone the process of symbolization. (PF 105)

By separating the subject from the maternal Thing, the Law produces the subject of lack. What remains of the Thing is the *objet a*. To understand how the *objet a* causes desire, consider the common observation that an individual tends to be attracted to the same kind of person. Why is that? Why do I find myself drawn to the same kind of person again and again? Some people have certain empirical features – tone of voice, eye or skin colour, facial gestures, certain dispositions and so on – that my mind unconsciously associates with my fantasy of fullness. Those empirical features embody for me the *objet a*. Insofar as they embody it, persons having those features will cause my desire for them. This entails Lacan's claim that 'there is no sexual relation'. Sex is for the subject a matter of trying to recover that lost part of itself that the other person embodies for it at the time. The other person is a means to the attainment of the subject's end. Sexual desire is narcissistic and fetishistic. It is about that part of the other person (the breast, the phallus, etc.) that causes the subject's desire, it is not about the other as a whole person. Put concretely, the *object* of my desire is this *woman*, but the *cause* of my desire are the *feature(s)* she possesses and that embody the *objet a*. In sex, you don't have two individuals attempting to complete each other. You don't have a relationship with another human being. There is the subject and the *objet a* embodied by the other person. The other person is for the subject like a dildo or sex doll. (Love is a different matter, although I don't propose to go into it.)

Attraction turns into repugnance when the subject realizes that the woman he desires is a substitute for the missing Thing and that she doesn't fill the void – that, in other words, she is 'trash' because she is not up to the task of being the Thing for the subject: she cannot make him whole again. The *objet a* (the representative of the Thing) frames the subject's desire. It is its fantasy of a recovered fullness and positivity, the fantasy causing desire. The critical usefulness of the concept of *objet a* is evident once we recognize that all ideology is a promise of fullness or of a reconquered identity.

We can speak of three types of object in Lacan:

(a) The *objet a*. As the McGuffin in Hitchcock, this is a non-present objet, a pure pretext to start the narrative. Its 'signification is purely auto-reflexive, it consists in the fact that it has some signification for others, for the principal characters of the story' (SOI 206).

(b) The symbolic object (the phallus or lack in the Other). This object circulates between subjects, it functions as an object of exchange and serves 'as a kind of guarantee, pawn, on their symbolic relationship' (SOI 206). A leftover of the Thing, it is a positive condition 'of the restoration of a symbolic structure: the structure of symbolic exchanges between the subjects can take place only insofar as it is embodied in this pure material element which acts as its guarantee' (SOI 207). What makes this object unique is that it represents the symbolic relations. It is not simply a part of the whole, it is a part that represents the whole. An indifferent, contingent material element sets in motion a symbolic exchange between subjects that previously had no relationships. This thing causes a symbolic order to spring up. It can do this because it embodies the lack in the big Other and organizes around it a signifying network.

(c) The third kind of object is neither the void left by separation from the maternal Thing nor a special kind of object of exchange, but a thing that insists in its material presence owing to the fact that it embodies maternal *jouissance*.

The subject presumed to . . .

The symbolic object is at work in the transference. The patient presumes that the analyst knows the meaning of her symptoms, that he is in possession of the missing phallus. 'This knowledge is of course an illusion, but it is a necessary one' (SOI 210). It is not possible to produce new knowledge – the knowledge of her symptoms – without this illusion on the part of the patient. Žižek adds to it the following three positions: there is the subject presumed to believe, the subject presumed to enjoy and the subject presumed to desire. I want to highlight several features of the last two in the remainder of this Section. The subject presumed to enjoy corresponds to the obsessional neurotic. The subject presumed to desire corresponds to the hysteric.

(a) The obsessional neurotic is someone who supposes that the big Other is in possession of a limitless *jouissance*, which he finds unbearable. In his mind, he has to save the Other from it. 'This supposed *jouissance* is one of the key components of racism: the Other (Jew, Arab, Negro) is always presumed to have access to some specific enjoyment, and that is what really bothers us' (SOI 212).

(b) The hysterical subject identifies with the Other who is supposed to know how to organize its desire. The question to ask the hysteric is not 'what does he desire?' but 'Where does he desire from? Who is the other person through whom he is organizing his desire?' (212). The hysteric depends on the Other to organize his desire.

The subject presumed to know (the meaning of the patient's symptoms) is the ground of the subjects presumed to believe, enjoy and desire. Let me conclude by noting in this connection some of the principal differences Žižek lists between obsessional neurosis and hysteria. These are to be understood not as clinical types so much as subjective positions, positions occupied by the subject in relation to the world. Let us keep in mind as well the critical significance of the hysteric's position vis-à-vis ideological interpellation discussed in Section 1.

- A hysterical symptom stages a repressed wish, an obsessional one the punishment for realizing it;
- A hysterical person cannot bear to wait, he misses the object of his desire by trying to get to it too quickly; the obsessional neurotic postpones, delays indefinitely;
- For the hysteric, the object procures too little enjoyment; for the obsessional neurotic, it procures too much enjoyment (which is why he keeps postponing his encounter with it);
- The hysteric asks the Other what it wants, uncertain as he is about his desire; the obsessional neurotic addresses this question to himself.

Žižek adds that we should not be misled by the impression of symmetry. The default position is that of the hysteric, whereas that of the obsessional neurotic qualifies it. For example, self-doubt is really though tacitly a doubt about the Other's desire; postponing the encounter with the object because it's unbearable is really a way of avoiding being disappointed about it and so on.

Žižek returns to the central claim concerning the undoing of our attachment to ideology, which consists in going through the fantasy, of recognizing that the *objet a* (which promises fullness) masks the lack in the Other.

Study questions

1. How does Žižek understand Lacan's claim that 'there is no metalanguage'?
2. What roles does the Real play in Žižek's theory of ideology?

Section 6

In the final Chapter, Žižek turns to Hegel in the background of Lacan's notion of the big Other. The central ideological gesture consists in presupposing that the big Other exists. It is the means by which the subject secures the consistency and meaning of its experiences. Žižek uses Hegel to show how this presupposition comes into effect.

In this Section, I explain some of the concepts in Kant and Hegel that Žižek draws on in the Chapter, particularly in relation to Hegel's *Lectures on the Philosophy of Religion*, his *Lectures on Fine Art* as well as his *Phenomenology of Spirit*. Žižek's appropriation of Hegel is heterodox and causes problems particularly when he tries to defend Yirmiyahu Yovel's reading of Hegel and, second, in his attempt to assimilate lack in Lacan with negativity in Hegel. I conclude the Section with a few study questions.

The indefinite judgement, lack and negation

In the next two sections, Žižek draws on Kant and Hegel in order to continue to specify his take on Lacan's notion of *objet a*. Key here is the notion of the indefinite or infinite judgement which Žižek refers to on a number of occasions in *The Sublime Object of Ideology* and other works (as in Chapter 3 of TN or Chapter 1 of PV). Aristotelian logic distinguishes between three kinds of judgement under the rubric of quality: the affirmative (S is P), the negative (S is not P) and the infinite or indefinite judgement (S is non-P).

- Socrates is mortal.
- Zeus is not mortal.
- Dracula is non-mortal.

The first affirms the predicate of the subject, the second denies it of the subject, whereas the third relates the subject to an indeterminate predicate. Non-mortal is not only the negation of what is mortal and immortal. It is also a positive state, that of being undead. It is indeterminate in its extent – and is thus called an indefinite or infinite judgement – because it doesn't demarcate a distinct class, that is, a class distinct from the class of all things mortal and immortal. In effect, as Žižek often emphasizes, to be undead (non-mortal) is a qualification of things whose default state is to be mortal. It demarcates an excess immanent to mortal beings that eludes the symbolic opposition between what is mortal and immortal.

It goes without saying that this isn't true of every possible predicate of an indefinite judgement, for example, the rose is a non-table. For Žižek, the two predicates of which it is true are 'non-mortal' and 'non-human', that is, to be undead and inhuman. The two of them represent that part of the subject it's had to renounce in order to gain entrance to the symbolic order: the *objet a* or maternal Thing, the Freudian drive. Put differently, there is no better predicate than 'being undead' or 'being inhuman' to describe the subject's experience of the drive: it is for it something monstrous and uncanny, without project or goals, implacable in its demand for satisfaction (*jouissance*). The drive is typically objectified as a living substance that lacks a distinct, recognizable (humanoid) shape, such as the alien in the film franchise *Alien* or Dracula in Bram Stoker's novel.

In Chapter 6 of *The Sublime Object of Ideology*, the infinite judgement marks out the sublime object (the *objet a*) that gives body to the subject understood as the empty place in the symbolic order.

> Thus the status of the sublime object is displaced almost imperceptibly, but none the less decisively: the Sublime is no longer an (empirical) object indicating through its very inadequacy the dimension of a transcendent Thing-in-itself (Idea) but an object which occupies the place, replaces, fills out the empty place of the Thing as the void, as the pure Nothing of absolute negativity – the Sublime is an object whose positive body is just an embodiment of Nothing. (SOI 234)

What is the sublime object displaced from and to what is it displaced? From Kant's understanding of it in the *Critique of Judgment* to Hegel's notion of the negating negativity of the subject, that is, its self-transcendence. For Kant, a sublime object is an empirical thing whose extent or might is for the subject infinite or boundless. In truth, however, in judging the object sublime, the subject makes an error. It attributes to the object a property that belongs to it, notably, its moral vocation. It projects the unconditionality of its freedom onto a natural thing. Certainly, images of a state of chaos in nature – or rather, of nature in a raw, wild state, earthquakes, a mountain ridge and so on – are sublime because they suggest something that transcends nature, the Idea of Reason as the Idea of the Unconditioned or Absolute, of, notably, Freedom, or, what amounts to the same thing, the noumenal thing or thing-in-itself. For Hegel, on the other hand, the thing-in-itself is an abstraction produced by the 'I' that bears the imprint of the subject. The crucial passage for Žižek's claim is to be found in Part I of Hegel's *Encyclopaedia of Philosophical Sciences.*

> The *thing-in-itself* (and here 'thing' embraces God, or the spirit, as well) expresses the ob-ject, inasmuch as *abstraction* is made of all that it is for consciousness, of all determinations of feeling, as well as of all determinate thoughts about it. It is easy to see what is left, namely, what is *completely abstract,* or totally *empty,* and determined only as what is 'beyond'; the *negative* of representation, of feeling, of determinate thinking, etc. But it is just as simple to reflect that this *caput mortuum* is itself only the *product* of thinking, and precisely of the thinking that has gone to the extreme of pure abstraction, the product of the empty 'I' that makes its own empty self-*identity* into its *ob-ject.*[1]

Hegel is saying two things. The first is that the thing-in-itself is the product of an abstraction. Withdraw from the object before you your thoughts, sensations and feelings about it. What you're left with is the empty thought of something in general – of something distinct from you. His second claim is that this concept of something in general bears the stamp of the subject's negativity, it is like a mirror that reflects its agency (the 'self-*identity*'). The thing-in-itself is but an objectification of the formal and empty identity of the subject, that is, of the subject thought abstractly. If you have an impoverished notion of the subject, expect to have an impoverished notion of the object, and vice versa – This is what Hegel is partly getting at. The crucial claim Žižek takes away from

Hegel is that the thing-in-itself is not an object external to the subject but is, instead, a part of the subject. It is the locus, in the subject, of what is 'undead' – that is, of the drive or its representative, fantasy or *objet a*. Žižek continues in the same paragraph:

> This logic of an object which, by its very inadequacy, 'gives body' to the absolute negativity of the Idea, is articulated in Hegel in the form of the so-called 'infinite judgment', a judgment in which subject and predicate are radically incompatible, incomparable: 'the Spirit is a *bone*', *Wealth* is the Self, 'the State is *Monarch*', 'God is *Christ*'. (SOI 234)

Not all of these judgements strictly qualify as examples of what Hegel calls an 'infinite judgment' in the Third Book of the *Science of Logic*. An infinite judgement for Hegel has a paradoxical character. It is a judgement that denies the very thing that constitutes a judgement, that is, the link connecting the subject and predicate. It is one in which 'the form of judgement is set aside'.

> It is supposed to be a *judgment*, and consequently to contain a relation of subject and predicate; yet *at the same time* such a relation is supposed *not* to be in it.[2]

'Spirit is not blue' is a good example. The judgement is correct, yet in spite of its correctness, it is absurd because it is not a judgement at all. We have two domains – Spirit and colour – that are unconnected with one another. Yet the copula 'is' produces the appearance of a connection. Be that as it may, it is clear what Žižek is trying to get at with his examples.

(a) His examples assert the *identity* of incompatible determinations, that is, of the spiritual with the natural, the nonsensuous with the sensuous. The copula is the 'is' of identity, not of predication. They look more like instances of Hegel's speculative judgement insofar as they assert the identity of identity and difference.

(b) For example, in 'Spirit is a bone', 'Spirit' is what remains identical to itself, 'bone' is a particularity and difference and so on.[3]

(c) The highlighted term in Žižek's examples doesn't principally denote the corresponding sensuous object. It is a *sinthome*, a signifier in

> which the signifying network is in suspense and that, as a result, insists in its sheer material presence. Žižek's claim is that this traumatizing signifier – '*bone*', '*Wealth*', '*Monarch*', '*Christ*' – is the repudiated locus of the subject's (Spirit's) enjoyment (*jouissance*). Such is 'the logic of sublimity' (the heading of the section). It elevates a contingent, sensuous object to the status of the Thing, that is, of a primally repressed signifier.

What I find questionable is Žižek's identification of lack in Lacan with spirit's negating negativity in Hegel. He writes: it 'fills out the empty place of the Thing as the void, as the pure nothing of absolute negativity'. Or as he puts it in *Enjoy Your Symptom! Jacques Lacan in Hollywood and Out*:

> Hegel radicalized Kant by conceiving the void of the Thing (its inaccessibility) as equivalent to the very negativity that defines the subject. (ES 137)

Of course, it is not so much Kant as Lacan that is at stake with this notion of 'the void of the Thing'. The reason I find it questionable is that they are not structurally homologous. The subject's *negating negativity* for Hegel doesn't have the status of the traumatic Real – of, that is, the impossible-unthinkable-unsayable kernel of the subject. On the contrary, negativity is what *brings out the rationality of what there is*. Let me explain.

Spirit's relation to what is other qualifies as a 'negation' because, merely by virtue of having a relation to an object, Spirit *distinguishes itself from it* and, thus, *at the same time posits it as other*. The subject doesn't have to be literally transforming the world by working on it in order to bring about meaning and rationality in it. The fatalist who accepts things as they are *determines* the given precisely as something accepted: the given is no longer merely given, it is no longer an immediate sensuous presence, it is *posited* by the subject as something accepted, as something of which it thinks 'So it is.' A thing becomes qualitatively other, it is transposed into a different set of relations (cultural-rational rather than simply natural-causal), the moment Spirit appears in Nature and the thing exists *for* it.

Negation means that Spirit is active in transforming what there is, including itself. At a very basic material level, the being of the subject is without inner positivity or content. It derives its entire content from the exteriority of the world, of the big Other, of language. Freedom, that is, rational self-determination, is the only thing that characterizes it at a purely formal level. It is what constitutes Spirit *qua* Spirit. Put differently, the properties I am born with and that I acquire socially – my race, gender, nationality – do not define me unless I define myself in their terms. The Hegelian subject *is* what it *takes itself to be*. I may have such-and-such properties. But they are *mine* – that is, they are constitutive of my identity – insofar as I determine myself on their basis. And the demand I put to others is not that they recognize the properties I identify with, but that they recognize my *agency*, that is, my capacity to rationally determine who or what I am, that is, what properties are mine.

In one sense, certainly, there is something abyss-like about self-conscious Spirit. Its characteristic freedom is unintelligible in natural-causal terms. It is a 'void' in the order of Nature. It is groundless from the point of view of empirical science. It is, however, self-grounding from the point of view of the cultural-intersubjective game we participate in of giving and demanding others for reasons for their actions and beliefs. It is self-grounding, that is, self-determining, because to be free is to justify one's actions and beliefs by reference to standards one is the author of. The norms by which we regulate social life are, according to Hegel and Kant, self-authored, whether or not we're aware of it.

Negation in Hegel is not what lacks the signifier. It is, on the contrary, the dialectical dynamic that *institutes* it. That is why after all the absurd judgement from the section of the *Phenomenology of Spirit* that deals with phrenology, 'the *being of Spirit is a bone*' (SOI 208), is eventually surpassed. It is thanks to its negativity that the subject uncovers the rationality of the world and that it makes explicit its symbolic organization.

Žižek's reading of Hegel is at odds with the contemporary reading of Hegel by the likes of Robert Pippin and Stephen Houlgate. That is of course not the problem. The problem is that some of what Žižek says about Hegel is hard to reconcile with what Hegel says in his text. As a result, it weakens the claims Žižek makes on behalf of Hegel.

Beauty and the sublime: The pleasure principle and its beyond

This is what the reader should keep in mind in her reading of Žižek's reading of Kant and Hegel on beauty and the sublime. Žižek starts Chapter 6 by addressing Yirmiyahu Yovel's discussion of Hegel's classification of what Hegel calls 'The Religions of Spiritual Individuality' in his *Lectures on the Philosophy of Religion*. The order in which Hegel presents them in his 1824 lectures is as follows:

(1) the Jewish religion as the Religion of Sublimity,

(2) the Greek religion as the Religion of Beauty, and

(3) the Roman religion as the Religion of Expediency.

All three come before Christianity. Their ordering is not incidental. According to Hegel's dialectical procedure, the last one contains the truth of the previous ones, whereas the earlier ones contain a partial take on the truth. That is why they are inevitably superseded – logically if not also historically – by the following ones, which have a more comprehensive take on the truth. ('Truth' for Hegel is not the property of a proposition but the Whole, the Absolute, which realizes itself in Nature and Spirit and whose realization Spirit recollects, inwardizes, in the system of philosophy.) The ordering of the three religions that come before Christianity is a *ranking*. The religions are ranked by reference to how they represent the truth, in this instance *spirit*, the *divine*, or *freedom* – terms that, in Hegel's vocabulary, are often synonymous.

For the purpose of clarity, let me add the following. In the *Lectures on the Philosophy of Religion*, Hegel distinguishes between the religions of nature ('Immediate Religion, or Nature Religion') and the religions of spirit ('The Religions of Spiritual Individuality'). The former have for their object the divine understood as an impersonal natural force, fire in Zoroastrianism, the sacred cow in Hinduism and so on. The latter conceive of the divine as a personal self-conscious power. Once again, this is a ranking. The religions of spirit have a more concrete understanding of the divine than the religions of nature. 'Concrete' doesn't mean material. It means inwardly differentiated.

The divine is grasped in terms of a multiplicity of attributes that are inwardly connected with one another. In other words, it is grasped as a self-conscious agency that relates to itself and posits its attributes as its own. Judaism along with the Greek and Roman religions and Christianity are religions of spirit in this sense.

Yovel claims that according to Hegel's own logic, the Jewish religion should follow the Greek and Roman ones, it should not come before them, because it gives a more adequate representation of Spirit as a self-conscious moral agency. Greek and Roman gods are not adequate representations of Spirit on account of their particularity and empirical content. The Jewish religion is the negation of the finitude of Nature. The Greek and Roman religions are religions of Spirit, it is true, yet they think of Spirit (the nonsensuous) in sensuous forms, whereas the Jewish religion raises Spirit above Nature: it is purely an object of thought, not an object of the senses. It posits it as an unconditioned, self-determining, free totality. Christianity is privileged on the ground that it affirms the unity of God with man, of the infinite with the finite.

> Hegel has here given way to his personal anti-Semitic prejudice, because to be consistent with the logic of the dialectical process it is undoubtedly the Jewish religion which should follow the Greek. (SOI 227)

It is possible to put matters as follows without betraying the spirit of Hegel's thought. Polytheism presupposes a trust in what the senses deliver as evidence for one's beliefs. It is not incompatible with the position of the empirical realist who thinks that physical objects exist independently of the mind and that they have the properties we see in them. From its point of view, what exists are discrete finite objects of Nature. Now the divine for the polytheist radiates in certain privileged physical objects, in idols, statues or dolls. The statue of Zeus at Olympia, for instance, is not for the Classical Greek and Plato's contemporary the symbol of an absent deity. The statue *is* the god. The god dwells in it and in the temple that houses the statue. It is a 'holy precinct'. Judaism might be thought of, in this connection, as the corollary sceptical attitude that calls into question the empirical realist's stance. It posits Nature as though it were an illusion and as lacking truth. Nature is not for Judaism an independent substance. It doesn't properly exist. It's dependent upon the Creator. The Creator exists because it is independent and infinite, a self-determining cause, a free moral and all-powerful agency. And precisely to the extent that the divine transcends the world of the senses, we find the prohibition in Judaism on making idols and copies of God. That is why Yovel insists that the Jewish religion should come after the Greek and Roman ones as their *negation*. Christianity would then be next in order as the religion that brings together the extremes of the Greek religion of beauty and the Jewish religion of sublimity, that is, as the *negation* of the first negation.

Žižek doesn't consider Hegel's *Lectures on the Philosophy of Religion* in his reading of Yovel. Had he done so, he would have noted from the table of contents that Hegel is uncertain about where to put Judaism in his classification of religions. In the 1824 lectures, he places Judaism before the Greek and Roman religions. In the lectures of 1827, he places Judaism *after* the Greek and before the Roman religion, whereas in the lectures of 1831, he places Judaism among the religions of nature (!) between Zoroastrianism and the Egyptian religion. This ambiguity speaks in favour of Yovel's claim.

What does Žižek do in support of Yovel? He draws on the concepts of beauty and the sublime. He writes that

> the very logic of the dialectical process compels us to conclude that Sublimity should follow Beauty because it is the point of its breakdown, of its mediation, of its self-referential negativity. (SOI 228)

Judaism, the religion of the sublime, ought to have followed the Greek religion, the religion of beauty. Why? Because the sublime is the breakdown of beauty. The facts, however, do not speak in favour of Žižek's claim, at any rate not in the way Hegel presents them in his *Lectures on Fine Art*. The sublime is the breakdown not of beauty but of the symbolic form of art. Hegel distinguishes between three forms: Symbolic, Classical and Romantic. The (nonsensuous) content of art is the same in each case. It is the Divine, Freedom or the Absolute. What distinguishes them is the (sensuous) form they use to represent it. Symbolic art uses naturally occurring forms like the sun or fire, or manmade items like buildings and monuments, architecture being its paradigmatic art. Classical art uses the human form to represent the divine, its paradigmatic art being sculpture, whereas Romantic art – where art ultimately transcends itself in the sphere of religion – uses the inwardness of spirit, communal feeling and cult to represent the divine; its paradigmatic arts being painting, music and poetry. Art in general – in its three forms – is intrinsically tied to the field of the sensuous, whereas religion transcends it in its representation of the divine. Religion, in short, is a more adequate representation of the truth.

The sublime is the breakdown of the Symbolic form art because it is the negation of its position. Symbolic art takes the divine to be some indeterminate sensuous thing, whereas the religion of sublimity claims that the divine is strictly nonsensuous. Classical art is a reconciliation of both positions. It claims that the divine is the unity of the sensuous and supersensuous in a privileged sensuous form, the human body. Why? Because there is no other naturally occurring form in the universe that represents the unity of soul and body. Now that is just what *beauty* amounts to for Hegel, this concordance of the sensuous with the nonsensuous in a unique sensuous form. Thus, at least from the point of view of the *Lectures on Fine Art,* it is perfectly justified – without there being an apparent hint of anti-Semitism – to say that Judaism is followed by the Greek religion, the religion of sublimity by the religion of beauty.

* * *

Let me highlight the interesting connection Žižek makes between beauty and the pleasure principle, on the one hand, and, on the other, between the sublime and the death drive. Beauty is linked to the pleasure principle because, after all, beauty is a source of pleasure, of, as Kant says in the third *Critique*, disinterested pleasure. We generally think of a beautiful work of art or of a beautiful scenery of nature as something that is pleasurable in itself rather than owing to what it brings to us or adds to our interest. But beauty also adds to our interest, and in this connection, it is not unrelated to the reality principle. For Lacan, the reality principle maintains the homeostatic balance of the organism; it is in the service of its welfare. Why is the sublime linked to the death drive beyond the pleasure principle? Because it produces pleasure in displeasure, that is, *jouissance*. The sublime object humiliates the subject because it is boundless in extent or power, it overwhelms its finitude.

> In short, the Sublime is 'beyond the pleasure principle', it is a paradoxical pleasure procured by displeasure itself (the exact definition – one of the Lacanian definitions – of enjoyment (*jouissance*). (SOI 228–9)

For Kant, a sensuous object that overwhelms the imagination is the index of a supersensuous Idea, of, that is, an Idea of Reason. The displeasure results from experiencing the limit of our imagination whereas the pleasure from the way this inadequacy, on the part of our imagination to grasp the whole, suggests another power in us that transcends Nature, notably, our moral agency.

Kant distinguishes in this connection between enthusiasm and fanaticism. The fanatic claims to be in direct communication with the Absolute beyond the empirical world. He claims to have an unmediated link to it. The enthusiast claims that our relationship to the Absolute is mediated by the sensible world – that we have a negative relationship to it: the thing-in-itself doesn't appear; however, its non-appearance makes itself felt (it does appear) in the failure of the power of imagination and in the ascendancy of the power of reason.

From Kant to Hegel: Lack and negativity

Žižek touches on one of the more complex themes in modern thought – that is, the transition from Kant's critical idealism to Hegel's absolute idealism – in order to account for the maternal Thing that resides in the subject. I have already expressed my reservation about the structural similarity Žižek posits between Lacan's notion of lack and Hegel's negativity. I leave that aside for now and attempt to clarify the paragraphs, in Chapter 6, that deal with this transition. They can be found on pp. 231–4.

According to Žižek, we can understand this transition in two steps. Let me start with the relevant passage related to the first one.

> Hegel's reproach to Kant (and at the same time to the Jewish religion) is, on the contrary, that *it is Kant himself who still remains a prisoner of the field of representation*. Precisely when we determine the Thing as a transcendent surplus beyond what can be represented, we determine it on the basis of the field of representation, starting from it, within

> its horizon, as its negative limit: the (Jewish) notion of God as radical otherness, as unrepresentable, still remains the extreme point of the logic of representation. (SOI 232)

One of the principal claims of Kant's critical idealism is that it is illegitimate for a cognitive judgement to transcend the boundaries of space and time. Space and time are *a priori* conditions of the possibility of empirical knowledge. The object of your judgement will lack a referent – you won't be talking about anything at all – unless you talk about something that possesses spatiotemporal properties. To talk of the soul, for instance, or of freedom or God, is empty. It is to employ concepts without the corresponding intuitions that give those concepts their object and reference. At the same time, space and time are subjective conditions of knowledge. That means that they are not mind-independent properties. In other words, Newton is wrong to think that space and time exist in themselves. They are forms of intuition exclusive to human knowledge. Non-human creatures may know in terms other than the intuitions of space and time.

The notion of a Thing-in-itself naturally follows from this critical restriction. If space and time do not exist in themselves but are necessary for us, then what exists in itself is non-spatiotemporal. Thus, the legacy of Kant's idealism is this split between the field of phenomena – that is, empirical objects in space and time to which the categories of the understanding apply – and the Thing-in-itself, that is, freedom, the soul and God. Although they are unknowable, they play a role in Kant's moral theory.

Hegel's criticism, as Žižek describes it, is that this distinction owes everything to one of the terms being distinguished. The Thing-in-itself is determined from the point of view of the field of phenomena. Put differently, Kant doesn't think of freedom (and the rest) on its own terms. He thinks of it from the point of view of natural necessity. Does Hegel regress to a pre-critical (pre-Kantian) standpoint by suggesting that we ought to speak of the Absolute as it were directly? Not at all. 'This is *not* Hegel's position: the Kantian criticism has here done its job and if this were Hegel's position, Hegelian dialectics would effectively entail a regression into the traditional metaphysics aiming at an immediate approach to the Thing' (SOI 232).

The second step consists in recognizing that if the Thing is unknowable, that is not because it is a transcendent cause, that is, a cause external to the field of phenomena. It is because the field of phenomena is inwardly split and bears witness to a *negativity and excess immanent to it*. Hegel posits the external difference between phenomena and the Thing-in-itself as an *internal* one, as a difference immanent to the field of phenomena. That is to say that the empirical world, or rather, its symbolic structure, is *in itself inconsistent and lacking*. For Hegel,

> there is *nothing* beyond phenomenality, beyond the field of representation. [. . .] The experience of the Sublime thus remains the same: all we have to do is to subtract the transcendent presupposition – the presupposition that this experience indicates, in a negative way, some transcendent Thing-in-Itself persisting in its positivity beyond it. In short, we must limit ourselves to what is strictly immanent to this experience, to pure negativity, to the negative self-relationship of the representation. (SOI 232-233)

The Thing is part of the phenomenal order (rather as the title 'Lenin in Warsaw' denotes a missing object that is part of the picture). Let us recall that Žižek is articulating, with the help of Kant and Hegel, the negativity in the symbolic order or the part of the subject in the Other that refers us to the Real of the drive. What makes the big Other (and the subject alienated in it) inconsistent is the fact that it is lacking and doesn't exist as a totality.

'Spirit is a bone'

What does Hegel mean when he says that 'the *being of Spirit is a bone*'? Phrenology in the *Phenomenology of Spirit* is part of the chapter where reason is certain of being at home in the physical world and where it aims to discover what it is by observing itself in it. It observes itself in the world (a) as a living body (biology), (b) as having customs and habits, passions and inclinations (psychology) and (c) as having a body that expresses the activity of the self (physiognomy, which Hegel understands as the study of what the self intends or means to say with its facial and other bodily expressions). Phrenology takes this last position to the extreme by insisting that there is a causal relation between the inner and outer. It claims that Spirit is localized in the brain and that the study of the skull – on which the brain has effects – informs us about the character of the self. The bumps and hollows of the skull reflect the temperament of the self that inhabits it. – It goes without saying that Hegel considers phrenology a pseudo-science and its claims to be foolish and absurd. The point is that the idea that the self is a bone is logically entailed by the position that defines the chapter, which is that Spirit is known by means of empirical observation. The section on phrenology can be thought of as a *reductio ad absurdum* argument. Phrenology is the *Aufhebung* of the entire shape of consciousness called 'Observing Reason'.

Now we know that Žižek takes Hegel's proposition in a quite different way and from a different angle. His aim is to illustrate Lacan's thesis that the repudiated locus of the subject's *jouissance* (the drive) takes the form of an inert material Thing, a signifier that instead of signifying, stubbornly insists in its material presence.

> We *succeed* in transmitting the dimension of subjectivity *by means of the failure itself*, through the radical insufficiency, through the absolute maladjustment of the predicate in relation to the subject. (SOI 235)

The bone with which Spirit is identified for Žižek is the *objet a*. Žižek's point is that the subject is characterized by an inner discord between the Symbolic and the Real – '*this negativity, this unbearable discord, coincides with subjectivity itself*' (SOI 235) – and, second, that the renunciation of the Real is the necessary condition of the advent of the subject. The subject comes into existence as a speaking being by foreclosing the Real: 'its limit is its positive condition' (SOI 236).

For Žižek, then, the bone is not a signifier, it doesn't represent Spirit, or rather, it is the signifier of lack and Spirit's immediate, non-signifying presence, the site of its traumatic enjoyment (*jouissance*). It is an objectification of the lack in the symbolic order and thus the very thing (or Thing) that initiates the process of symbolization.

> The bone, the skull, is thus an object which, by means of its *presence*, fills out the void, the impossibility of the signifying *representation* of the subject. In

> Lacanian terms it is the objectification of a certain lack: a Thing occupies the place where the signifier is lacking. (SOI 236)

The reason why it doesn't signify – the reason why it insists in its material presence – is that it makes up for a loss that cannot be named. The 'bone' is where we have to situate the repressed unconscious. It is a primally repressed signifier.

Hegel's *Phenomenology of Spirit* and the heroism of flattery

In the section titled 'Wealth is the Self', Žižek focuses on the chapter of Hegel's *Phenomenology of Spirit* titled 'Self-Alienated Spirit. Culture.' Žižek's focus is on Hegel's statements on language, specifically Hegel's view that to speak is to utter a universal, which betrays one's intention of saying or meaning something particular (providing that that is one's intention). I covered this point in an earlier Section. Žižek is emphasizing a theme we are already familiar with. This is that if we want to get the subject into our line of sight, then we must start with language rather than with some psychological interiority, that is, with an intention, meaning or idea. From a purely linguistic-structuralist point of view, the subject is an empty form, it has the form of a signifier that lacks a signified (no signifier adequately defines it).

Before I say something about the chapter in Hegel's *Phenomenology of Spirit* under consideration in 'Wealth is the Self,' let me give it a context by saying a word or two about Hegel's *Phenomenology of Spirit*, what it's about and how it proceeds. Generally speaking, it describes various forms of consciousness. A form of consciousness is a relation between a subject and an object in which the subject takes the object to be so-and-so and then finds that its conception of the object is called into question by its experience of it. The dialectic is an ongoing process in which the subject

(a) sets up a standard of truth (a conception of the object), then

(b) has an experience of the object in light of that standard, and then

(c) finds that standard wanting, that is, it doesn't match its experience of the object.

That leads to the breakdown of the corresponding form of consciousness. In the next form, we have a subject with a new standard of truth or conception of the object, one that is a revision of the first. And the whole thing starts over again. The dialectical process is a progress. It goes on until the subject's *conception* of the object and its *experience* of it match one another. When they finally coincide at the end of the *Phenomenology of Spirit*, we have the identity of thought and being – we have the consciousness that the structures of the world are identical with the structures of mind, identical not in substance but in form. That is to say, they are rational through and through. At that level, philosophy proper – the *Science of Logic* – begins. From that point on, it becomes both possible and necessary to carry out a deduction of the categories, that is, of the forms of rationality common to both mind and world. Hegel's is a revisionary project of Kant's transcendental deduction of the categories in the first *Critique*.

In the subsection of 'Self-Alienated Spirit. Culture' that Žižek reads and that is titled 'Culture and its realm of actuality', we have a form of consciousness where the subject relates to two social institutions: the state and wealth. Or again, we have a subject with two kinds of interests, political and corporate (economic). The subject can relate to both of them in two ways:

(a) I can identify with state power and wealth. For example, I can say that my essence lies in the royal state and in wealth. That is the consciousness of *nobility*.

(b) I can find myself alienated from both of them. For example, I can say that state power is oppressive and that wealth, though instrumentally a good, is an evil because I don't have any. That is the *base* or *ignoble* consciousness.

The dialectic shows the collapse of (a) into (b). The historical background to this section is the late feudal period and the institution of absolute monarchy with King Louis XIV, the Sun King who said 'I am the state.' Thus, France from the fifteenth to the early seventeenth century. Hegel's main interlocutors are Montesquieu's political reflections and Diderot's *Rameau's Nephew*.

The noble is a vassal. He is an advisor to state power. The world he creates is feudalism. Consider what is implied by nobility. What must it do to maintain itself? In a word, it must sacrifice itself for the state. It must show that it has no particular interests, that its only interest is the universal, the King or the State, and it can show this in the final analysis by choosing to die for it. That is 'the heroism of service'.

If the nobleman remains alive, then the suspicion arises that he has particular interests after all. To convince the King, the nobleman's heroism of service must be supplemented by the heroism of flattery. Such flattery must prove that state power is absolute and that the nobleman owes everything to it, including its self or 'I'. How does the heroism of service become the heroism of flattery? Through language. The self can sacrifice itself without losing itself through language. The nobleman proclaims to the Sun King, 'you are everything and I offer myself to you, great King'. He performs the customary ritual of obeisance. Žižek's point is that it doesn't matter whether the nobleman is being insincere at heart. The truth lies on the side of the signifier, not on that of the nobleman's meaning or intention. When I speak and say 'I,' I present a self that is void of inner psychic contents. The 'I' is an *indexical without material reference*, that is, without reference to some psychic substance, much like 'This', 'Here', 'Now'.

> The 'truth' of what we are saying depends on the way our speech constitutes a social bond, on its performative function, not on the psychological 'sincerity' of our intention. [. . .] The flattery achieves a radical voidance of our 'personality'; what remains is the empty form of the subject – the subject as this empty form. (SOI 239-240)

The 'heroism' Žižek insists on lies in the use of language. When I speak, it's as if my interiority were sacrificed and what remains is an empty-formal 'I'. *Subjectivity is a formal-linguistic construct.* Put differently, the subject is a function of the symbolic order that masks its lack or nonexistence (as a totality). Žižek returns to this at the end of the text.

The 'beautiful soul' and positing the presuppositions

The central insight of the final sections of the text is Žižek's reading of the Hegelian notion of positing the presuppositions. Žižek shows that this is the ideological gesture *par excellence*. Let me get there one step at a time.

He begins by exemplifying it through the beautiful soul in Hegel's *Phenomenology of Spirit*. This is a form of consciousness that appears in the third subsection of the chapter titled 'Spirit that is certain of itself. Morality'. The subsection is titled 'Conscience. The 'beautiful soul,' evil and its forgiveness'. The main interlocutor in the subsection is Fichte and his notion of conscience.

Conscience is a form of consciousness meant to resolve some of the difficulties encountered in Kant's moral theory, specifically (though not only) the opposition between the two classes of motivations in Kant's theory of action. According to Kant, either you act for the sake of duty or as reason commands or you are motivated by self-love, self-interest, your welfare or the welfare of your own. There is no third source of motivation. Further, Kant claims that these two sources are irreconcilable. Furthermore, suppose you're a shop-owner and that you've decided, as your maxim and rule of action, generally not to lie to your customers. Kant claims that it is impossible to know whether you've chosen not to lie because duty so commands or because it serves your interest not to lie. Your motivation is inscrutable. In what sense does conscience resolve these problems?

Very simply, conscience is certain that what it does fulfils duty. An immediate (non-inferential) inspection of its contents certifies that it does what duty bids. Conscience is a *self-certifying moral agency*. It takes itself to be the ultimate moral authority. Acting dutifully doesn't mean doing this rather than that. It means being convinced of the rightness of your action, whatever you do. Conscience makes its conviction public by expressing it. It takes its own inner voice to be absolute and divine. And in this context, everyone acknowledges the equally inviolable authority of all.

The 'beautiful soul' is the consciousness that contemplates this purity of its self. It withdraws from the world, from action and language, in order to sustain its purity. The world would taint it. Naturally, the dialectic shows that it is inwardly empty and that its words are hollow.

Now Žižek suggests that the falsity of the beautiful soul doesn't lie in its inactivity or refusal to engage in the world. It consists

> in the very mode of activity implied by this position of inactivity – in the way the 'beautiful soul' structures the 'objective' social world in advance so that it is able to assume, to play in it the role of the fragile, innocent and passive victim. (SOI 244)

Let us keep in mind the distinction Žižek draws here between two kinds of act:

(a) I can bring about a change in the physical world by acting on it. We might call this an intervention in the empirical order of things where I causally bring about some change.

(b) There is the framework, setting or situation in which I act or do something: I do not act in a vacuum. Further, this framework is not some natural scenery that is there willy-nilly like the passing clouds. It is instituted by the subject and accepted or rejected or altered by the newcomer. I accept or reject how the situation must be understood in which I act. Or I seek to alter its terms. At stake is a symbolic act, that is, an act that relates to the symbolic order, that effectively institutes or modifies it.

According to (a), I act on some pre-existing material object. According to (b), I act on the symbolic coordinates that structure the situation where I find myself face to face with some material object. According to the former, I produce a material effect. According to the latter, I alter the meaning of the situation. I posit the presuppositions structuring the setting of my action at (b).

> the real act is of a strictly symbolic nature, it consists in the very mode in which we structure the world, our perception of it, in advance, in order to make our intervention possible, in order to open in it the space for our activity (or inactivity). The real act thus *precedes* the (particular-factual)

> activity; it consists in the previous restructuring of our symbolic universe into which our (factual, particular) act will be inscribed. (SOI 245)

'Precedes': it is *a priori*, it is logically prior to the factual-empirical act. It is its framing. Consider the mother who complains that she does everything for her family and gets nothing in return, that her life is an endless devotion and sacrifice. This silent sacrifice 'is her imaginary identification: it gives consistency to her self-identity – if we take this incessant sacrificing from her, nothing remains; she literally "loses ground"' (SOI 245). This identification sustains her social relations with her family members. If she were to sacrifice her position as victim exploited by her family, she would dissolve its social relations.

> The mother's fault is therefore not simply in her 'inactivity' in silently enduring the role of exploited victim, but in actively sustaining the social-symbolic network in which she is reduced to playing such a role. (SOI 245)

From the standpoint of her family, she appears to herself likeable in her (imaginary) role as passive victim. To change things, she'd have to give up her imaginary identification and alter the symbolic coordinates structuring the relations between her family members.

What does it mean 'to posit the presuppositions'? It is a formal act for which the subject is responsible or guilty. It is the act of converting the *given* into the *posited*, of altering 'this is the way things are' into 'this is how they are for me (or us)'. It is to transform what exists in itself into something that exists for us. Žižek's claim is an *a priori* one. In order to act in the world, I must take myself to be responsible-guilty for its setting. *I must take the world to be in a certain condition or state if I am to act in it.* This 'taking' is a formal-symbolic activity. It doesn't change the content of the situation, only its meaning. As a Kantian might say, you must posit a conceptual framework in order to be able to perceive and act on empirical things. There's neither seeing nor acting in a symbolic-conceptual vacuum.

This is what separates Hegel from Marx according to Žižek. The subject for Marx transforms the world by working on it. His empirical activity transforms the given and makes of it something posited. It becomes a *result* of human activity, and that result is the manmade presupposition of any future activity.

For Hegel, it is the other way around. Before the Marxist subject is able to transform the world by working on it, he must already have posited it, he must have made himself responsible for its symbolic structure. The given must already have been framed by the subject as something-to-be-transformed-by-labour. The 'subject *pretends* that the reality which is given to him in its positivity – which he encounters in its factual substantiality – is his own work' (SOI 248). In one sense, the formal act of positing the presuppositions doesn't do anything. It doesn't effect a material change. That is why Žižek says that it is a pretence. In another sense, however, its symbolic effect is infinitely more profound than a change in the material order of things. Think of the custom of burying and mourning the dead. Hegel talks about it in connection with Polynices' burial in Sophocles' *Antigone* in the chapter of the *Phenomenology of Spirit* titled 'Spirit', in the subsection 'The ethical world. Human and Divine Law: Man and Woman.'

> This universality which the individual *as such* attains is *pure being, death*; it is a state which has been reached *immediately*, in the *course of Nature*, not the result of an action *consciously done*. The duty of the member of a Family is on that account to add this aspect, in order that the individual's ultimate being, too, shall not belong solely to Nature and remain something irrational, but shall be something *done*, and the right of consciousness be asserted in it. [. . .] Blood-relationship supplements, then, the abstract natural process by adding to it the movement of consciousness, interrupting the work of Nature and rescuing the blood-relation from destruction; or better, because destruction is necessary, the passage of the blood-relation into mere being, it takes on itself the act of destruction.[4]

The upshot of Hegel's claim is that the practice of mourning and remembrance turns what is in actual fact a natural occurrence – someone's death – into a conscious achievement and event of symbolic-communal significance. By remembering-internalizing the deceased, the family member wrests him from Nature and he becomes an ancestor or god, a permanent member of the community, an object of reverence and respect, a guide or role-model and so on. Žižek relates it to Lacan's notion of the forced choice where we assume as our own what is given to us anyway – our nationality, sex, race and the like.

Such acts in which the presuppositions of a situation are posited are speech acts. They institute a different way of understanding a situation. Think of the priest who says 'You are now husband and wife' before the congregation. He alters the presuppositions under which we must henceforth understand any kind of exchange between the man and the woman.

> This 'empty gesture' receives from Lacan its proper name: the signifier; in it resides the elementary, constitutive act of symbolization. (SOI 251)

The act of symbolization and subjectivity coincide. Perhaps nothing better exemplifies what the subject at bottom consists of than the monarch. The monarch doesn't do anything. He simply adds his name to the laws his ministers proposed and debated. The subject is a formal act without content.

> The Monarch is thus a subject par excellence, but only in so far as he limits himself to the purely formal act of subjective decision: as soon as he aims at something more, as soon as he concerns himself with questions of positive content, he crosses the line separating him from his councillors, and the State regresses to the level of Substantiality. (SOI 252)

To symbolize is to assume responsibility for the content, it is to accept or reject it, it is to make it one's own or disown it. The signifier is, in this respect, all-determining.

Let me conclude by citing the concluding sentences of Žižek's book:

> What is the 'empty gesture' by means of which the brute, senseless reality is *assumed*, accepted as our own work, if not the most elementary ideological operation, the symbolization of the Real, its transformation into a meaningful totality, its inscription into the big Other? We can literally say that this 'empty gesture' *posits the big Other, makes it exist.* (SOI 262)

Why is the formal act of positing the presuppositions the ideological act *par excellence*? Because it is tantamount to supposing that the big Other exists. In supposing that it exists, the subject secures the meaning and consistency of its experiences.

It is against this background that we can understand why Žižek privileges a figure like Antigone that exemplifies symbolic suicide. Symbolic not actual suicide. Someone who kills herself supposes that the big Other exists. Her suicide is an address to the Other. Symbolic suicide is a different kind of thing. It annuls your place in the symbolic network. It is tantamount to excommunication. The reason why such an agent (of the drive) fascinates is that she cancels the presupposition of the big Other. For her, the big Other doesn't exist. She undermines the founding ideological gesture (see EN 58–59). She accepts 'the Real in its utter, meaningless idiocy'. She keeps open 'the gap between the Real and its symbolization' (SOI 263) – the very gap that makes possible radical democracy.

Study questions

1. How does Žižek interpret Hegel's claim in the *Phenomenology of Spirit* that the 'Spirit is a bone'?
2. Why is 'positing the presuppositions' the central ideological gesture for Žižek?

4

Reception and influence

There is little doubt that when future philosophers and historians will write the history of ideas of the twenty-first century, they will see its first two decades marked by the contribution of Žižek's unique brand of Lacanian reading of films, novels, political events, cultural and philosophical texts. His first book in English, *The Sublime Object of Ideology*, published in 1989, is a landmark contribution in relation to Ernesto Laclau and Chantal Mouffe's discourse theory. One of its main critical merits lies in rehabilitating a version of the Marxist notion of ideology after the Foucauldian and Derridean critiques that saw it as bound up with a hopeless essentialism and a questionable distinction between science (knowledge) and ideology.

The growing influence of Žižek's thought can be measured by the increasing number of textbooks that have arisen on it in the last two decades, including Ian Parker's *Slavoj Žižek – A Critical Introduction* (London: Pluto Press, 2004), Rex Butler's *Slavoj Žižek – Live Theory* (London and New York: Continuum, 2005), Marcus Pound's *Žižek: A (Very) Critical Introduction* (Grand Rapids, MI: Wm B. Eerdmans, 2008), Matthew Sharpe and Geoff Boucher's *Žižek and Politics: A Critical Introduction* (Edinburgh: Edinburgh University Press, 2010), Sean Sheehan's *Žižek: A Guide for the Perplexed* (London and New York: Continuum, 2012) and Kelsey Wood's *Žižek: A Reader's Guide* (Oxford: Blackwell, 2012), to name just these. A good number of edited volumes on Žižek's thought have also appeared since the mid 2000s, as well as a reader comprising Žižek's essential texts (until 1999) titled *The Žižek Reader*. It is edited by Elizabeth Wright and Edmond Wright (Malden, MA, USA;

Oxford, UK; Carlton, Victoria, Australia: Blackwell Publishing, 1999). Finally, an online peer-reviewed journal devoted exclusively to the study of Žižek's thought, titled *International Journal of Žižek Studies*, appeared in 2007.

Žižek's influence has been felt in theology primarily thanks to such works of his as *On Belief* (London: Routledge, 2004), *The Fragile Absolute or, Why is the Christian Legacy Worth Fighting For?* (London, Verso 2001), *The Puppet and the Dwarf: The Perverse Core of Christianity* (Cambridge, Massachusetts, London, England: The MIT Press, 2003), *The Monstrosity of Christ: Paradox or Dialectic?* (Cambridge, Massachusetts, London, England: The MIT Press, 2009) co-authored with John Milbank, *Paul's New Moment: Continental Philosophy and the Future of Christian Theology* (Grand Rapids, MI: Brazo Press, 2010) co-edited with Creston Davis and John Milbank and *God in Pain: Inversions of Apocalypse* (New York: A Seven Stories Press, 2012) co-authored with Boris Gunjevic.

Žižek's principal contribution is his Lacanian theory of ideology. It has proven influential in many areas in the humanities and social sciences, including anthropology, literary studies and film theory (see the recent *Political Theory and Film: From Adorno to Žižek* by Ian Fraser [London and New York: Rowman & Littlefield, 2018] and Matthew Flisfeder's *The Symbolic, the Sublime, and Slavoj Žižek's Theory of Film* [New York: Palgrave Macmillan, 2012]), critical theory and political theory, media studies (see Paul A. Taylor's *Žižek and the Media* [Cambridge, UK: Polity, 2010] and *Žižek and Media Studies: A Reader* edited by Matthew Flisfeder and Louis-Paul Willis [New York: Palgrave Macmillan, 2014]), and psychoanalysis. There are a good number of journal articles on fetishism that draw directly on Žižek's reflections on the topic in Marx, Freud and Lacan in *The Sublime Object of Ideology*. An edited volume has recently appeared to mark Žižek's contribution in literary theory. It is titled *Everything You Always Wanted to Know about Literature but Were Afraid to Ask Žižek* and edited by Russell Sbriglia (Durham and London: Duke University Press, 2017).

The Sublime Object of Ideology is a challenging work with original insights on Marx, Lacan, Kafka, Freud, Brecht and many more. It is a major philosophical text and, as is usually the case with such texts, we should expect its future readers not only to produce radically divergent readings – some might see it as a work of metaphysics, others as one in the field of anthropology or of critical theory or of psychoanalysis and so on – but to unearth insights not yet available to today's scholarship. And what is true of the interpretation of a symptom is true of the interpretation of *The Sublime Object of Ideology*: the future will decide what it will have meant.

Finally, let me mention Žižek's recent engagement with the new materialisms and realisms in continental philosophy in the Introduction to the volume *Subject Lessons: Hegel, Lacan, and the Future of Materialism*, co-edited with Russell Sbriglia (Evanston, Illinois: Northwestern University Press, 2020). Žižek engages head-on with these two related movements that have been mounting an attack against the cultural materialism in the human and social sciences informed by Foucault and Althusser. These include Bruno Latour's actor-network theory, Ray Brassier's speculative realism and Graham Harman's and Levi Bryant's object-oriented ontology. The materialists think that what there is consists of matter understood as self-organizing (rather than as a passive, inert substance). They want to see cultural studies turn from an exclusive focus on texts, discourses, ideological state apparatuses and so on to the material reality that is independent of human thought. Žižek doesn't disagree. The problem with new realism and object-oriented ontology according to Žižek is that they miss their target. Their target isn't different from cultural materialism. On the contrary, they take charge against what Quentin Meillassoux calls 'correlationism', the notion that the subject and object are inter- or co-dependent. Their aim is to overcome both in the direction of an inquiry of what things are in themselves, that is independent of what they are for human thought. They take aim at the very subject that cultural materialism takes aim. This is the conscious subject, reason, free will, the thinking ego. Now we know that psychoanalysis shows this subject to be the plaything of its unconscious thoughts (signifiers). This is why the target for Žižek is not the conscious mind but the subject of the unconscious.

Like them, however, Žižek maintains that reality is ontologically incomplete. He proposes that there is a virtuality in matter. Drawing on a certain reading of Hegel, he says that matter is incomplete and inconsistent and that it contains the potentials for the genesis of the subject. The inconsistency and incompleteness of matter is correlative to subjectivity. His claim is that the subject of the unconscious – more particularly the drive (the Real) – is what makes reality, the in-itself, incomplete.

> the true way to be a consequent materialist is not to directly include the subject into reality as merely one object among others, but to bring out the Real of the subject, the way the emergence of subjectivity functions as a cut in and of the Real.[1]

This further explains the meaning behind Žižek's charge that the new realists and materialists have an allergy to the Lacanian Real. His claim is that it is not enough to think of the subject as a thing among things rather than as a transcendental-constitutive subjectivity endowing what there is with meaning. The degree zero of subjectivity is the traumatic Real healing itself. Language, 'reason', the symbolic order – what are they if not a symptom of the body, the subject's way of healing from the trauma? In failing to note the Real in the subject, they fail to note the thing that constitutes the subject, that is, the traumatizing encounter with the signifier. It splits the subject and lodges, in fantasy, the *objet a* that would complete it.

Notes

Chapter 1

1 Žižek's reading of Foucault is not accurate. The late Foucauldian subject does not create herself. Foucault doesn't fall back on this humanist model. The technologies of the self do not replace disciplinary mechanisms. They unsettle their control.

2 Ernesto Laclau, 'The Impossibility of Society', *Canadian Journal of Political and Social Theory* 15, no. 1–3 (1991): 22.

3 Ibid., 24.

Chapter 2

1 Slavoj Žižek, 'Beyond Discourse-Analysis', in *New Reflections on The Revolution of Our Time*, ed. Ernesto Laclau (London and New York: Verso, 1990), 249.

2 Ibid., 250–1.

3 Ibid., 252.

4 Ibid., 253.

5 Ibid., 251.

6 Sigmund Freud, words added by me.

7 Freud, *Interpretation of Dreams*, 474.

Section 1

1 This is what Butler misses in her exchange with Žižek and Laclau, namely, the fact that the formal and the *a posteriori* do not mutually exclude one another. See CHU.

2 Žižek often though not only directs this criticism against feminists who historically relativize the structure of the Oedipal organization of the subject.

3 Peter Sloterdijk, *Critique of Cynical Reason, Theory and History of Literature*, Vol. 40, trans. M. Eldred (Minneapolis and London: University of Minnesota Press, 2001), 5.

4 Ibid.

5 See David Foster Wallace, 'E Unibus Pluram: Television and U.S. Fiction', *Review of Contemporary Fiction* 13, no. 2 (1993): 151–94.

6 Don DeLillo, *White Noise* (London: Picador, 2011), 365–6.

7 Louis Althusser, *Lenin and Philosophy and other Essays*, trans. B. Brewster (New York and London: Monthly Review Press, 1971), 161.

8 Ibid., 174.

9 Immanuel Kant, 'Critique of Practical Reason', in *Practical Philosophy*, trans. M. J. Gregor (Cambridge and New York: Cambridge University Press, 1999), 191; 5:64.

Section 2

1 See also Collete Soler, 'The Paradoxes of the Symptom in Psychoanalysis', in *The Cambridge Companion to Lacan*, ed. J.-M. Rabaté (Cambridge: Cambridge University Press, 2003), 86–101.

2 Jacques Lacan, 'The Subversion of the Subject and the Dialectic of Desire', in *Écrits, The first Complete Edition in English*, trans. B. Fink (New York and London: W.W. Norton & Company, 2006), 681–2.

3 Ibid., 580.

Section 3

1 See, for instance, Johann Gottlieb Fichte, *Addresses to the German Nation*, ed. G. Moore (Cambridge: Cambridge University Press, 2009), 102–3, *et passim*.

2 See Claude Lefort, 'The Permanence of Theologico-Political?', in *Democracy and Political Theory*, trans. D. Macey (Cambridge: Polity Press, 1988), 213–55.

3 John Searle sees it precisely as a story or picture rather than as a theory. See John Searle, *Intentionality: An Essay in the Philosophy of Mind* (Cambridge: Cambridge University Press, 1999).

4 Jacques Lacan, *Transference, The Seminar of Jacques Lacan Book VIII*, trans. B. Fink (Cambridge: Polity Press, 2015), 143 (words added by me).

5 Sigmund Freud, *The Standard Edition of The Complete Psychological Works of Sigmund Freud, Volume VII (1901-1905), A Case of Hysteria, Three Essays on Sexuality and Other*

Works, trans. J. Strachey (London: Vintage, The Hogarth Press, and The Institute of Psycho-Analysis, 2001), 223.

6 Jean Laplanche, *New Foundations for Psychoanalysis*, trans. D. Macey (Cambridge and Oxford: Basil Blackwell, 1989), 126.

Section 4

1 See Walter Benjamin, 'Theses on the Philosophy of History', in *Illuminations*, trans. H. Zohn (New York: Schocken Books, 2007), 253.

2 Ibid., 255.

3 Ibid., 260.

4 Ibid., 261.

5 Ibid., 254.

6 Ibid., 262–3; words added by me.

7 Ibid., 261–2; words added by me.

8 Ibid., 263.

Section 6

1 G. W. F. Hegel, *The Encyclopaedia Logic (with the Zusätze), Part I of the Encyclopaedia of Philosophical Sciences with the Zusätze*, trans. T. F. Geraets, W. A. Suchting, and H. S. Harris (Indianapolis and Cambridge: Hackett Publishing Company, Inc., 1991), 87.

2 G. W. F. Hegel, *Hegel's Science of Logic*, trans. A. V. Miller (New York: Humanity Books, 1999), 642.

3 Žižek recognizes this later in the chapter. See SOI 235.

4 G. W. F. Hegel, *Hegel's Phenomenology of Spirit*, trans. A. V. Miller (Oxford: Oxford University Press, 1977), 270–1.

Chapter 4

1 Russell Sbriglia and Slavoj Žižek (ed.), Subject Lessons: Hegel, Lacan, and the Future of Materialism (Evanston: Northwestern University Press, 2020), 13.

Select Bibliography

Althusser, L. (1971), *Lenin and Philosophy and Other Essays*, translated by B. Brewster, New York and London: Monthly Review Press.

Benjamin, W. (2007), 'Theses on the Philosophy of History', in H. Zohn (trans.), *Illuminations*, pp. 253–64, New York: Schocken Books.

DeLillo, D. (2011), *White Noise*, London: Picador.

Fichte, J. G. (2009), *Addresses to the German Nation*, edited by G. Moore, Cambridge: Cambridge University Press.

Freud S. (2001), *The Standard Edition of The Complete Psychological Works of Sigmund Freud, Volume VII (1901–1905), A Case of Hysteria, Three Essays on Sexuality and Other Works*, translated by J. Strachey, London: Vintage: The Hogarth Press, and The Institute of Psycho-Analysis.

Hegel, G. W. F. (1991), *The Encyclopaedia Logic (with the Zusätze), Part I of the Encyclopaedia of Philosophical Sciences with the Zusätze*, translated by T. F. Geraets, W. A. Suchting, and H. S. Harris, Indianapolis and Cambridge: Hackett Publishing Company, Inc.

Hegel, G. W. F. (1997), *Hegel's Phenomenology of Spirit*, translated by A. V. Miller, Oxford: Oxford University Press.

Hegel, G. W. F. (1999), *Hegel's Science of Logic*, translated by A. V. Miller, New York: Humanity Books.

Kant, I. (1999), *Practical Philosophy*, translated by M. J. Gregor, Cambridge and New York: Cambridge University Press.

Lacan, J. (2015), *Transference, The Seminar of Jacques Lacan Book VIII*, translated by B. Fink, Cambridge: Polity Press.

Laclau, E. (1990), *New Reflections on The Revolution of Our Time*, London and New York: Verso.

Laplanche, J. (1989), *New Foundations for Psychoanalysis*, translated by D. Macey, Cambridge and Oxford: Basil Blackwell.

Lefort, C. (1988), 'The Permanence of Theologico-Political?', in D. Macey (trans.), *Democracy and Political Theory*, Cambridge Polity Press.

Searle J. (1999), *Intentionality: An Essay in the Philosophy of Mind*, Cambridge: Cambridge University Press.

Sbriglia, R. and S. Žižek (ed.) (2020), *Subject Lessons: Hegel, Lacan, and the Future of Materialism*, Evanston: Northwestern University Press.

Sloterdijk, P. (2001), *Critique of Cynical Reason, Theory and History of Literature*, Vol. 40, translated by M. Eldred, Minneapolis and London: University of Minnesota Press.

Soler, C. (2003), 'The Paradoxes of the Symptom in Psychoanalysis', in J.-M. Rabaté (ed.), *The Cambridge Companion to Lacan*, 86–101, Cambridge: Cambridge University Press.

Wallace, D. F. (1993), 'E Unibus Pluram: Television and U.S. Fiction', *Review of Contemporary Fiction*, 13 (2): 151–94.

Index

agalma 74, 75
agency 3–5, 8, 10–11, 20, 30, 37, 49, 67, 69–70, 78, 81, 154
alienation 4–5, 33, 76, 86, 118, 124, 144, 147
Althusser, Louis 1–4, 6, 23, 36–9, 41, 45, 47, 49, 63, 90, 157, 160
analysand 55, 59, 84
antidescriptivism 70–3
antidescriptivist 66, 71–3, 75
anti-essentialism 8
Antigone 12, 43, 99, 152, 154
Aristotle 4, 73
Aufhebung 145

baptismal act/ceremony 71–2
Benjamin, Walter 101–5, 107
big Other 3, 5–6, 11, 17, 20, 23, 32–4, 36–7, 41–2, 45–6, 48, 50–1, 55–6, 58–9, 61, 67, 72, 79, 81–2, 84–6, 88–9, 91, 96, 99, 124, 127, 129–30, 132, 137, 144, 153–4
bourgeois formal democracy 68
Butler, Judith 44, 159

capitalism 1, 5, 26, 69, 102
caput mortuum 134
castration 23, 32, 39, 88, 96–7, 114, 116, 119–20, 123, 126
categorical imperative 12, 42, 64
Che vuoi 82, 85–6
combination and substitution 28, 63
constitutive act of symbolization 153
constitutively open 28, 120
critique of ideology 4, 15–17, 30–1, 47, 49, 55, 68, 89–90

das Ding 128
death 12, 21, 39, 43, 50, 58, 61, 63, 92, 94–101, 108, 110, 113, 141, 152
definiens 66
DeLillo, D. 3, 34, 160
democracy 8, 11, 18, 20, 68, 70, 77, 92, 109–10, 154
Derrida, Jacques 9, 94, 111, 113–15, 117, 125
descriptivism 71
desire 2–3, 16, 19, 42, 52–3, 56, 59–60, 66, 74–6, 79, 82–3, 85–90, 118, 120, 124–5, 128–31, 160
diachronic function 54
dissemination 111, 113–14

ecologism 67–8
ego ideal 80
empirical obstacle 29, 90, 118
empirical realism 93
enjoyment (*jouissance*) 17, 22–3, 41, 46, 48–51, 59–65, 67, 80–1, 87–91, 95, 118, 120, 130–1, 136, 142, 145
essence 5, 9, 11, 37, 72–7, 94, 147
essentialism 8, 70, 77, 155
eternal nature 122
evil 122–3, 147, 149
evolutionary idealism 100
excitations 13, 23, 82, 88
extimacy 43, 95

false consciousness 9–10, 30–1

fantasmatic 68, 74, 76
fantasy 23, 29, 39–41, 44–5, 48, 50, 55–9, 61–2, 74, 79, 82, 85–7, 90–1, 97, 118–19, 123, 128–9, 131, 135, 159
fascism 67, 77
fascist ideology 64
feminism 19, 67–8, 77, 159
fetishism 27, 32, 156
fetishistic tendency 27
formula of ideology 33
Foucault, Michel 1–4, 16, 98, 125, 157, 159
freedom 5, 7, 9, 12, 48, 120, 122–3, 134, 137–8, 140, 143
Freud, Sigmund 11–12, 15–16, 21–3, 37, 39–40, 46, 49–52, 57, 61, 63, 82, 86, 105, 118–19, 124, 156
Freudian drive 11–12, 42–3, 133
fundamental fantasy 57, 59

general equivalent 26
general will 68
graph of desire 52–3, 79, 83, 88, 90

Habermas, Jurgen 1–4, 16
Hegel, G. W. F. 1, 13, 19, 56, 92–3, 102, 127, 132–47, 149, 151–2, 154, 157, 161
Heidegger, Martin 5, 95
historical materialism 92, 101
historical materialist 102–4, 107
historical necessity 56–7
historical rupture 49, 54
historical subject-positions 126
history 5, 7, 36–7, 56, 68, 71, 96, 100–4, 106–8, 110, 155
homogeneous continuum 102
hypnotic voice 87
hypotactic 113
hysteria 42, 45, 46, 50, 84, 130

ideal ego 5, 80, 81
identity 2–4, 6, 9–10, 18–20, 28, 37, 44–5, 68–9, 72–7, 91, 111, 125–7, 129, 134–5, 137, 147, 151
identity of incompatible determinations 135
ideological field 69
ideological gesture 29, 132, 149, 154
ideology 48–9, 55, 62, 64–6, 68, 74, 77–8, 89–92, 109, 116, 120, 129, 131, 156
imaginary identification 5, 80–1, 151
imagined object 97, 100
immanent blockage 91
immanent unfolding 99
immaterial corporeality 27
inassimilable remainder 123
interpellation 3–6, 23, 36–8, 41, 45, 79, 84–5, 90, 131

Je ne sais quoi 72, 74, 86
Jetztzeit 92, 103–5, 107

Kafka, Franz 43, 63, 156
Kant, Immanuel 42–4, 64, 81, 105, 122–3, 132, 134, 136–8, 141–4, 149, 160

Lacan, Jacques 2, 5–6, 10, 16, 18–20, 23, 28, 32, 37–40, 42–3, 49–52, 54–6, 59–63, 66, 74, 79–82, 85–7, 89, 92–7, 101, 105–7, 111, 113–18, 120, 124, 128–9, 131–2, 136, 141–2, 145, 153, 156, 160
lack 17, 20, 23, 29, 36, 39, 41, 44, 46, 55, 59–61, 75–6, 84–6, 89, 94, 96–7, 100, 106, 113–16, 118–20, 123–4, 126–9, 131, 132
Laclau, Ernesto 7–11, 15–16, 18, 20, 44, 49, 66–70, 77, 90, 155, 159
language 17, 21, 39, 53–4, 70, 74–6, 93–4, 100, 111–18, 120, 125–6, 137, 146, 148–9, 158
(the) Law 32, 41–4, 46, 57–8, 63–4, 128
Lefort, Claude 70, 92
Leibniz, G. W. 104
liberalism 65, 67, 102

Marx, Karl 7, 16, 26–8, 69, 77, 101, 151, 156

master-signifier 49, 54
materialist creationist 100
maternal thing 87, 117, 126, 128, 129, 142
Maugham, Summerset 121
Messianic 105, 107
metonymic associations 113
metonymy 28
mirror phase (or stage) 38, 80
misrecognition 4–5, 23, 36, 38, 58–9, 79, 81
money 26–8, 60, 120
Mouffe, Chantal 7–8, 15–16, 18, 20, 44, 49, 66–70, 77, 90, 155

necessary limit 29, 90, 118
Nietzsche, Friedrich 1, 3, 16
nonsensuous 26, 135, 139–41

Objet (petit) a 19–20, 22–3, 56, 59, 61, 68, 73–4, 76, 85–7, 116–18, 128–9, 131–3, 135, 145, 158
obsessional neurotic 130–1
occasioning cause 52
Oedipal complex 42, 46, 89, 96, 159
overidentification 47

paratactic 113
pathogenic effect 56, 95–6
performative utterance 39, 74
phallus 32–3, 36, 42, 89, 96–7, 113–16, 120, 128–30
phantasmic 78
pleasure 12–13, 15, 19, 21–3, 32, 35, 39, 43, 46, 48, 63–5, 84, 87, 94–5, 105, 128, 138, 141–2
Point de capiton 53–64, 114
politics 7–10, 69, 110
positing the presuppositions 149–54
psychoanalysis 8, 13, 19, 33, 36, 41, 51, 59, 65, 115, 120, 156–7
psychobiological 84
psychotic 2, 9, 32, 95

quiddity 73
quilting-points 68, 90

race 6, 35, 69, 81, 137, 153
racism 67, 85, 130
(the) Real 4, 6–8, 11, 15–18, 20, 23, 39–40, 42, 44–5, 49, 51, 57, 66, 70, 76, 79–81, 87, 92, 95, 97, 99, 107–9, 111, 114, 116–20, 123–4, 126–7, 131, 144–5, 150, 153–4, 158
Reductio ad absurdum 145
reflexive relation to desire 124
regulative idea 68
repressed wish 50–1, 62, 131
retroactive constitution 107
retroactive effect 54, 73, 75, 120, 121, 123
retroactivity 49, 50, 52
rigid designator 73, 74, 76

Schelling, Friedrich Wilhelm Joseph 122
sensuous 26, 42, 135–6, 139–42
signifying network 95, 124, 129, 136
sinthome 51, 62, 63
Sloterdijk, Peter 30, 36, 160
social imaginary 61–2
social-immaterial quality of money 28
socialism 77
society 3, 8–12, 16, 18, 28–33, 36, 38–9, 42, 48, 54, 60–1, 63, 68–71, 79, 90–1, 109, 127
Sohn-Rethel, Alfred 29
Sophocles 43, 99, 152
stochastic process 109
subject of enunciation 52
subject of the statement 53
subjectivation 3–4, 20, 48, 126
subjective destitution 3–4, 12
sublime material 27
sublime objects 26
sublimity 136, 138, 140–1
substitute satisfaction 39, 50–1, 84
substratum 94
Sujet d'énoncé 125
superego 37, 46, 80
surplus of senseless traumatism 41
symbolic art 140

symbolic death 95, 99
symbolic existence 81, 97, 99
symbolic framework 51, 57, 98, 106
symbolic identification 6, 78, 80–2, 84
symbolic reality of subjects 119
symbolic suicide 3, 154
symptom 17, 19, 21, 31, 39–41, 45, 49–52, 55–6, 61, 63, 65, 90–1, 96, 105–6, 130, 131, 157–8
syntactic 111
syntagmatic and paradigmatic 28, 94

Tarski, Alfred 112
temporal idealism 51
theology 101–2, 156
thrownness 5
totality 8–11, 28, 36, 44, 48, 55, 68, 70–1, 89–91, 107, 127, 139, 144, 148, 153
transference 55–6, 58, 60, 130
transworld identity 76
traumatic encounter 124
traumatic limit 99
traumatic symptom 52
traversing the fantasy 40, 56, 58, 61

unbearable lack in the other 97
(the) unconscious 26, 36–7, 40–1, 50, 52–3, 55, 62, 82, 84, 95, 117, 119, 123, 125, 157–8
unconditional 12–13, 16, 22, 41–4, 58, 60, 63–5
unconditional imperative 43, 65
unconscious fantasy 62, 118–19
unconscious illicit wish 123

Zeitgeist 62